Harvard
Business
Review

ON

LEADING IN TURBULENT TIMES

THE HARVARD BUSINESS REVIEW PAPERBACK SERIES

The series is designed to bring today's managers and professionals the fundamental information they need to stay competitive in a fast-moving world. From the preeminent thinkers whose work has defined an entire field to the rising stars who will redefine the way we think about business, here are the leading minds and landmark ideas that have established the *Harvard Business Review* as required reading for ambitious businesspeople in organizations around the globe.

Other books in the series:

Other books in the series (continued):

Harvard Business Review on Innovation

Harvard Business Review on the Innovative Enterprise

Harvard Business Review on Knowledge Management

Harvard Business Review on Leadership

Harvard Business Review on Managing Diversity

Harvard Business Review on Managing High-Tech Industries

Harvard Business Review on Managing People

Harvard Business Review on Managing Uncertainty

Harvard Business Review on Managing the Value Chain

Harvard Business Review on Managing Your Career

Harvard Business Review on Marketing

Harvard Business Review on Measuring Corporate Performance

Harvard Business Review on Mergers and Acquisitions

Harvard Business Review on Negotiation and Conflict Resolution

Harvard Business Review on Nonprofits

Harvard Business Review on Organizational Learning

Harvard Business Review on Strategic Alliances

Harvard Business Review on Strategies for Growth

Harvard Business Review on Turnarounds

Harvard Business Review on Work and Life Balance

Harvard Business Review

ON

LEADING IN

TURBULENT TIMES

A HARVARD BUSINESS REVIEW PAPERBACK

Contents

Harvard
Business
Review

ON

LEADING IN TURBULENT TIMES

Moving Upward in a Downturn

DARRELL RIGBY

Executive Summary

AS THE RECENT BURSTING of the new economy bubble has shown, business cycles are still with us. The
question, then, is, what executives should do to help
their companies weather these downturns.

As in so many instances, there are conventional
approaches that appear to make sense in the short term.
But while these approaches seem reasonable in the heat
of the moment, they can eventually damage competitive
positions and financial performance.

Drawing on extensive research of *Fortune 500* companies that have lived through industry downturns and
economic recessions over the past two decades, Darrell
Rigby, a director of Bain & Company, reveals how companies need to go against the grain of convention and
exploit industry downturns to harness their unique opportunities for upward mobility.

1

The author explains that every downturn goes through three phases. He examines each phase and shows how successful players navigate the huge waves of a downturn. Smart executives, he says, don't panic: they look bad news in the eye and institutionalize an approach to detecting storms. Rather than hedge their bets through diversification, they focus on their core businesses and spend to gain market share. They manage costs relentlessly during good times and bad. They keep a long-term view and strive to maintain the loyalty of employees, suppliers, and customers. And, coming out of the downturn, they maintain momentum in their businesses to stay ahead of the competition they've already surpassed.

Every industry will face periodic downturns of varying severity, says Rigby. But executives with the vision and ingenuity to take unconventional approaches can buoy their companies to new heights.

Downturns are a recurring fact of life in every industry. Sooner or later, demand for an industry's products or services declines—often dragging prices down along the way—regardless of the state of the economy as a whole. While it's true that many more industries suffer downturns during recessions, it's a mistake to think that any industry is safe during periods of normal economic growth. In the past two decades, at least 20% of all U.S. industries have battled a downturn in any given year but 1984, when GDP growth soared to more than double the norm.

Given these apparently gloomy facts, what should executives do to help their companies weather a slump? As in so many instances, there are conventional approaches that appear to make sense in the short term. For example, company leaders often approach impending trouble with overconfidence, denying that their industry faces any real danger. Then, when the downturn is an established fact, they make across-the-board cuts of everything from R&D spending to employee head count. Finally, when signs of recovery are everywhere, they turn on the spending spigot to rebuild morale. Although these approaches seem reasonable in the heat of the moment, they can eventually damage competitive positions and financial performance.

Better outcomes are possible, however, if a company's leaders exploit industry downturns to harness their unique opportunities for upward mobility, the same way *Apollo 13*'s astronauts exploited the moon's gravitational pull to escape disaster. Both Arrow Electronics and Emerson (formerly Emerson Electric), for example, followed this path to emerge stronger following downturns. In the late 1980s, financially troubled Arrow launched a series of audacious but intelligent acquisitions during an industry downturn that allowed it to increase sales by more than 500%, turn operating losses into profits, and seize market leadership from a competitor that was once twice its size. Emerson, too, pressed ahead with an investment in a major air-conditioning-processor plant in Thailand during the Asian economic crisis of the late 1990s. While competitors mothballed projects, Emerson ramped up production, exported the plant's products, and secured a strong position for itself in the Asian market when the crisis ended.

To understand how successful companies combat declines in demand, Bain & Company analyzed 377 *Fortune* 500 companies that lived through industry slumps and economic recessions over the last two decades and interviewed nearly 200 of their senior executives. The research found that a downturn evolves through three separate phases. An examination of these phases reveals both the pitfalls that come from following conventional approaches and the rewards that can be reaped by exploiting contrarian opportunities. (See "Navigating a Downturn" for a review of these phases.)

Successful players in a downturn place counterintuitive bets in order to dramatically transform their market positions, but these bets are not lucky gambles that miraculously win big against the odds. Instead, they are rigorous and systematic moves that shift the odds in management's favor.

The Gathering Storm

In phase one of a downturn, storm clouds are gathering on the horizon, but industry executives are still basking in memories of sunny years of profitable growth and public accolades. Confidence remains high. As the clouds roll in, however, analysts report that industry growth is slowing, and divisional presidents signal that they might miss their budgets—while still beating the competition, which is doing even worse. Our research found two conventional approaches to such news. Many executives take few if any precautions; they simply act as if the storm will blow over. Others run for cover, investing in new and often unrelated businesses to hedge their bets. But smart executives resist those extremes: they prepare for the worst while focusing their companies on what they do best.

Once an industry is in the middle of a downturn, it is almost impossible for companies to come up with inventive solutions.

Navigating a Downturn

	The Conventional Approach	The Contrarian Approach	Success Stories
1. Storm Clouds on the Horizon	Express confidence that *your* industry (or *your* company) is safe from harm.	Build contingency planning into your culture and you'll be prepared for anything.	*Emerson, which reforecasts major financial drivers every month.*
	Hedge your bets: diversify in the hope that your winners will offset your losers.	Play to win where you are strongest: reinforce your core.	*Borden in the 1980s, which beat competitors by going on a strict corporate diet. (Like so many dieters, Borden put the weight back on in the late 1980s, and its performance suffered.)*
2. Battling the Elements	Cut costs like there's no tomorrow.	Treat your stakeholders like fellow combatants who happen to be stuck in the same foxhole.	*Solectron, which actually increased its focus on quality—its source of competitive advantage—during the recession of the early 1990s.*
	On the line in the budget for acquisition, write "$0."	Scoop up bargains that bolster the core business.	*Arrow Electronics, which has followed a "buy in bad times" strategy to become number one in its industry.*
3. Here Comes the Sun	Spend your way back into the good graces of employees and customers.	Don't overstress the engine: shift smoothly into higher levels of growth.	*Emerson, which handled phases one and two deftly during the recession of the early 1990s, steadily added people, R&D dollars, and capacity to maintain growth.*
			American Express, meanwhile, stumbled badly during the early 1990s. But it used the more forgiving post-recession climate to completely retool its business.

PREPARING FOR THE WORST

As evidence gathers that a downturn is likely, executives often continue to radiate confidence—and even clairvoyance—about the future. They don't want to frighten the troops, which will only make matters worse. Our research shows that most executives are likely to be overly optimistic in the face of an approaching downturn. Some will contend that their industries are safe, period. Others believe that their own company's ability to weather a downturn is superior to that of competitors. As a result of these misguided views, few companies have contingency plans in place that are ready for implementation.

One common concern is that contingency planning will signal a lack of confidence in the company's ability to grow and will thus dampen the organization's morale. Managers also worry that the process will be a waste of time that involves conjuring doomsday scenarios that may never materialize. But these concerns are short-sighted. Failing to plan for the worst is a much bigger mistake than upsetting the troops in the short term, because once an industry is in the middle of a downturn, it is almost impossible for companies to come up with inventive solutions.

Research shows that executives close their minds to new ideas when they are under stress. They tend to reach for the same levers they have pulled in the past, even if those levers don't work in the new conditions. The time to get a range of options out in the open, where they can be broadly and creatively debated, is before a downturn. Managers who are able to successfully negotiate a downturn build contingency planning into the culture of their strategic planning and budgeting processes.

Emerson has been one of the most consistent performers in the *Fortune* 500—it has seen 43 consecutive years of earnings growth—and its performance is the direct result of sophisticated planning systems. Former CEO Charles Knight and his senior managers spent at least half their time planning, and David Farr, who replaced Knight in the fall of 2000, has continued to build on Knight's foundation.

At Emerson, each unit must create a monthly report that reforecasts the remaining quarters of the current year as well as the first quarter of the next fiscal year. The monthly reports have been in place for 25 years but are continually refined. Each report includes a five-column table that lists growth projections and results. The first column displays current expected revenue and profits for the year and by the quarter. The second column shows expected revenues and profits from the previous month's report. The third shows the annual budget, and the fourth indicates actual revenue and profits for the previous year. The fifth column shows the expected percentage increase or decrease over last year's figures. "When I was a division president, I spent one day a month figuring out what would go into that report," says Farr. "The whole organization works that way—everyone who provides input to a division head spends one day per month focused on the future of the business. So if anyone sees a weakness, a plan to deal with it is immediately created."

Farr combines information from the monthly reports with that gathered during monthly one-on-one conversations with company business leaders at St. Louis headquarters. Emerson also holds annual planning conferences, during which each division must demonstrate how it will achieve sales and profit growth, regardless of conditions in the global economy or the industry. If the economy slows, Emerson's planning process allows the company to react quickly to protect sales and profits. As a result of all this planning, managers know far in advance of turbulence that if their business environment changes, they have a well-developed plan to deal with it. In the late 1990s, Emerson was able to sustain investment in next-generation process automation—the software and devices that regulate refineries, paper mills, and other industrial plants—while competitors focused on weathering the downturn. So when industry capital spending rebounded, Emerson emerged a stronger player, with sales and profits recovering several quarters ahead of the competition.

FOCUSING ON THE CORE

Here's another piece of conventional wisdom for surviving a downturn: hedge your bets. Pursue growth through diversification. Although this approach works well for individual investors, it makes little sense for corporations.

Contrary to conventional wisdom, downturn winners avoid diversification—and wisely so, because during downturns, typical diversification (the type that enters new businesses with low odds of achieving market leadership) is worse than worthless. It dilutes the company's average market share and therefore subjects it to more earnings volatility, not less. What does make sense is focus, creating ballast by reinforcing the core business. Successful downturn managers avoid diversification and concentrate as many resources as possible on playing to win on their main field of competition.

The example of Borden illustrates the pitfalls of diversification and the wisdom of focusing on core strengths. As the economy started to turn sour in 1980, CEO Eugene Sullivan put Borden, a sprawling $5 billion conglomerate at the time, on a strict diet. He divested the company of high-fat holdings unrelated to the core dairy business, including women's clothing operations, a phosphate rock mine, and a perfume company. Between 1980 and 1985, Sullivan also led the acquisition of 28 companies that were directly related to Borden's core business. As a result of these initiatives, the company's average annual net income was significantly higher than that of competitors throughout this period.

Unfortunately, Sullivan's successor, Romeo Ventres, reversed course: he acquired 90 grocery product companies, which distracted Borden away from its core dairy business. Borden became a jumble of consumer businesses that were spread much too thin across too many lackluster segments, and it was eventually scooped up by RJR Nabisco for $2 billion in stock.

Just as most people on the road assume that they're above-average drivers, most executives feel that their company will do better than competitors when faced with a decline in demand. But without proper planning, that's unlikely. When the weather starts to turn nasty, you can't wait until the last minute to buy batteries and water—by then, the shelves will be empty. Far better to plan ahead and stay focused on what you know you can do, not on what you hope to do better than established players in other markets.

Eye of the Hurricane

At a certain point, questions about an industry downturn become moot. No one can ignore the high winds or copious precipitation falling from the sky. Several smaller competitors are visibly on the brink of ruin. Investor dollars, management talent, and public attention are all seeking higher ground in industries with brighter prospects. Analysts aren't sure how long the downturn will last but express their fears that the industry will never be the same again. Companies think first and foremost about survival. Conventional wisdom urges quick and drastic action and cautions against acquisitions spending. Clearly, this is a time when costs must be reined in—but prudently. Smart companies look beyond the storm and even find ways to grow while it rages around them.

SEEING BEYOND THE BAD TIMES

When an industry's news is universally bad, managers tend to want to apply quick fixes. To cut costs quickly and spread the pain as fairly as possible, they slash budgets and staff across the board. They slice sales and earnings targets. They also reduce capital expenditures, drop services that competitors don't offer, and push suppliers to cut prices. In other words, their focus becomes short-term survival.

This is not unreasonable. Aggressive cost management is extremely important during a downturn, just as it is during an upturn. The problem is, many executives overreact to disturbing economic reports. Layoffs, for example, are often implemented as a way of holding down costs, but do they really make financial sense? Consider that voluntary employee turnover averages 15% to 20% per year in the United States, that sales volume was depressed by less than 10% in 85% of all industry downturns from 1977 to 1999, and that the average recession during that period lasted only 11 months. Given those facts, you have to wonder why there is such a scramble to fire—and then rehire and retrain—so many employees.

Squeezing suppliers is another short-term fix that can do more harm than good. Consider the tale of two Chryslers. During the recession of 1990 and 1991, Chrysler's approach was brilliant. Rather than forcing suppliers to share the pain, the company developed closer relations with them, outsourcing more components, reducing inventory, and slashing cycle times. If suppliers suggested ways to cut costs by 10%, they got half the savings. Chrysler used improved cash flows to invest in new product development, introducing cross-functional platform teams to improve quality and speed. Partly as a result of its work with suppliers—as well as judicious cost cutting—Chrysler was the only Big Three automaker to turn a profit in 1992.

Over time, Chrysler's hard-won cost advantage slipped, and now a different story appears to be in the making. The cornerstone of the current turnaround attempts is a supplier squeeze. Since January 1, 2001, all suppliers have been required to tear up existing contracts, reduce prices by 5%, and figure out how to cut an additional 10% from prices by 2003. Some suppliers are suggesting that they may withhold parts, and others have said they no longer have any incentive to bring Chrysler their best technologies. As a result of its tough stance, Chrysler may end up paying much more than it saves.

Contrarians know that downturns don't last forever and, in effect, they make friends with others who are trapped in the same foxhole—employees, vendors, business partners, and customers.

Costs do have to be carefully managed, but the key is consistency. A company shouldn't act one way in good times and another way in bad times. Otherwise, employees, suppliers, and other business partners will lose confidence in the company, and morale, cooperation, and productivity will all decline.

Now look to the contrarians. They know that downturns don't last forever and, in effect, they make friends with others who are trapped in the same foxhole—employees, vendors, business partners, and customers. They know that forcing a relatively small price cut (which will be remembered when the tables are turned) on suppliers is typically far less valuable than working with them to eliminate duplicate operations, improve forecasts, reduce inventories, and improve cycle times. They understand that although employee layoffs will reduce costs in the short term, the combination of severance expenses, loss of knowledge and trust, and subsequent hiring, training, and retention costs can quickly overwhelm expected savings. Companies such as Southwest Airlines, Harley-Davidson, and FedEx have no-layoff policies. As a result, their employees dig in during tough times rather than shop for new jobs.

Some companies have used downturns to build loyalty with other stakeholders. For example, electronic components manufacturer Solectron used the recession of the early 1990s to build customer loyalty. It did so by maintaining an unwavering focus on quality, the driving force behind its ability to attract and retain such customers as IBM, Hewlett-Packard, and Sun Microsystems. When demand fell in 1991, it increased its focus on quality and customer retention by interviewing customers weekly to check satisfaction. The company also added low-cost capacity in Malaysia that year to gain market share. These efforts during a downturn paid off handsomely: in 1991, Solectron won a Baldrige Quality Award, increased revenues by more than 50%, and replaced SCI Systems as the market leader. By focusing on the long term, Solectron has outperformed its competitors for more than a decade. Even as the industry slumps again this year, analysts predict that the company will grow 70% faster than SCI Systems between 2000 and 2002.

SHOPPING FOR BARGAINS

Conventional wisdom says that acquisitions are too risky to undertake during a downturn. According to this way of thinking, companies that appear ripe for the picking are likely to be deeply troubled and could drag down an already fragile business. Moreover, a company thinking about acquisitions may find that its cash is limited, that debt is unavailable, and that its stock price is depressed and thus not valuable as acquisition currency. Given these dismal conditions, the last thing a company should do is double down existing bets with acquisitions.

In keeping with this logic, only 20% of executives in our survey said they would be likely to make acquisitions during a future downturn, while 50% said they would be unlikely to do so (the rest were undecided). But clear winners in a downturn don't lock their purses; they spend on bargains, as the following example demonstrates.

In May 1985, the electronic components industry had hit a wall. It marked the beginning of a three-year slump that nearly drove Arrow Electronics into the ground. "We had $30 million worth of interest due that year and no operating income," CEO Steve Kaufman tells us. "We were losing big chunks of cash." Sales were collapsing, dropping from $730 million in 1984 to $550 million in 1987. Kaufman had already disposed of the company's sideline businesses in lead smelting and electrical distribution.

Although Arrow was number two in the industry, it was about half the size of the leader in the field.

Rather than cut back in the hope of surviving, Kaufman took advantage of the turbulence. "We made our greatest strategic moves during the period of greatest financial weakness," he says. He decided to get out of the hole through acquisitions. In 1987, Arrow bought the number three player. It funded the purchase with one-third Arrow stock and two-thirds cash that was borrowed against the acquisition target's receivables and inventory. One competitor snickered that the deal looked "like two men who can't swim grabbing each other in the deep end of the pool." But it worked. In the first full year after the acquisition, Arrow registered a modest net profit of $10 million. In 1991, Kaufman bought the new number three company, which was suffering during what turned out to be a little blip of an industry downturn. The deal was an exact replica of the 1987 acquisition. After several more acquisitions in Europe, Arrow swept past Avnet, the industry leader, to take the top position in the field. Kaufman looks upon the inevitable downturns in the electronic components business as an opportunity: "We acquire in bad times," he says. The surprising insight is that—assuming the core business is worth holding and growing—focused acquisitions during downturns should reduce risk, not increase it. As the Arrow example demonstrates, consolidating acquisitions diminishes business risk by strengthening the core and reducing earnings volatility.

Clear Skies on the Horizon

In the final phase of a downturn, portents of economic renewal emerge. Industry analysts begin to predict a turnaround, although they may be vague about the timing. Competitors start to take advantage of lowered interest rates to expand capacity and boost inventories in anticipation of rising sales. New orders start to flow in, and hitting next year's budget figures seems realistic. Conventional wisdom says that companies should make an abrupt about-face and shift into high-spending mode. But again, this is flawed advice. Companies that have successfully managed the first two phases of a downturn won't need to put the pedal to the floor. Those that remain beleaguered should consider completely overhauling the way they do business.

Failure to strengthen a company during a downturn can leave it in a much tougher position afterward.

ACCELERATING SMOOTHLY

Preparing to exit a downturn is either the easiest or the hardest stage of management. Companies that properly managed the first two phases of a downturn seldom need much advice in the third. They have mapped out and implemented contingency plans to deftly sidestep unexpected hazards. They have pruned share-diluting businesses and strengthened their core. They have bolstered vital relationships with employees, vendors, business partners, and customers. They have made share-boosting acquisitions at attractive prices. As a result of these moves, they have captured a disproportionate share of industry growth and profits. Now they are prepared to accelerate gradually and reap the rewards.

As the recession of 1990 and 1991 wound down, Emerson smoothly ramped up from a sales decline of 2% in 1991 to growth rates of 4% in 1992 and on to 16% by

1995. CEO Knight has steadily added people, R&D dollars, and capacity to maintain the company's return on assets at between 9% and 11% every year since 1990.

But Emerson's success is uncommon. In fact, more businesses fail after a downturn than during one. Part of the reason is that it takes a while for downturn-diseased companies to die. But a bigger part of the reason is that actions taken during the exit phase are inadequate to position the company for renewed growth.

COMPLETELY RETOOLING

After a painful time, executives often hope they can mend the damage by flipping on the spending switch. Their rationale is simple: since draconian cuts have seriously damaged the loyalty and morale of beleaguered employees, generous spending is now essential to regain their affections. In addition, heavy marketing, promotion, and service investments are needed to win back customers who defected when they grew exasperated with quality reductions and service cutbacks. Unfortunately, as companies in the motor vehicle and oil and gas industries have discovered, spending increases in this situation often outpace growth, forcing companies to make drastic cuts again when the next downturn hits.

Companies that fell behind in the first two phases require serious rehabilitation in this last phase if they hope to survive another downturn. Rather than try to spend their way out of their misery, troubled companies should consider retooling altogether. Such retooling may require a mix of the approaches outlined earlier but on a greater scale, from jettisoning noncore businesses to slashing costs. The difference is the warmer business climate: as industry conditions improve for what could be several years of growth, down-and-out companies have a better chance of successfully reinventing themselves.

American Express followed this path after emerging from the recession of the early 1990s in very poor shape. Strong new competition had led to a 1.6 million decline in the number of AmEx cards in circulation, and those who kept their cards were using them less and less. In 1991, about 100 restaurants in Boston threatened to boycott AmEx in protest over unreasonable transaction fees. Compounding these problems, the company had to write off $265 million in bad loans made to customers of American Express's credit card offering, Optima.

In 1993, the AmEx board ousted chief executive James D. Robinson III. Robinson's successor, Harvey Golub, set about rehabilitating and reshaping the company to take advantage of the expected upswing in consumer spending and prepare it for future slowdowns. He began by divesting noncore businesses like Shearson, a brokerage firm. Then he attacked costs, seeing the advantage of making the company lean in good economic times. By 1994, he had cut $3 billion in costs, along with 15,800 jobs. Although such pruning was painful, it prepared the company to grow as it recovered from the troubles of the early 1990s. If such drastic measures had been taken during a downturn, they would have hampered the company's ability to return to profitability. They might have destroyed the confidence of AmEx's organization and shareholders, eventually requiring even more dramatic actions and leading the company on a downward spiral.

Golub's third campaign was to refocus AmEx on its core business—charge and credit cards. For example, he successfully challenged the elitist attitude in the company that opposed allowing customers to use AmEx cards at gas stations. He also broadened the pool of retailing partners, signing up Kmart in 1993 and Wal-Mart in 1995.

As a result of these forceful measures, the company came back strong during good economic times. In 1994, the number of cards in circulation began to increase, rising from about 25 million to more than 29 million by 1996. The company introduced many new products, building its market share from 17% in 1994 to almost 21% in 1998. Its stock outperformed the S&P index by three-and-a-half times between December 1991 and the end of the decade.

As the story of American Express demonstrates, failure to strengthen the company during a downturn can leave it in a much tougher position afterward. At that point, dramatic changes will likely be required. The company may need to refocus on its core, prune its portfolio, and bring in new management, not only to bring fresh energy and breakthrough perspectives, but also to convince key stakeholders (especially employees) that the reinvention is for real. The new team needs to establish a core set of values and make it clear that the company will adhere to them in good times and in bad. To avoid wild spending swings, it has to establish cost structures that can be sustained through a downturn.

And then, after several years of profitable growth and public accolades for the management team, economic storm clouds will enter the scene . . . again. But the company will be much better positioned this time to handle the bad weather.

Look to the Lighthouse

Making it through the three phases of a downturn isn't easy, and there's no guaranteed path to success. Nevertheless, our research findings may provide a beam of light to help companies see their way through a storm. Companies that successfully navigate huge waves tend to look bad news in the eye and institutionalize an approach to detecting storms. Rather than hedge their bets through diversification, they place a big bet on their core businesses and spend to gain market share. They manage costs relentlessly during good times and bad. They maintain a long-term view and strive to earn the loyalty of employees, suppliers, and customers. Coming out of the downturn, they maintain momentum in their businesses to stay ahead of the competition they've already surpassed.

As the recent bursting of the dot-com bubble has shown, business is still subject to cyclical change. Every industry will face periodic downturns of varying severity. Executives with the vision, ingenuity, and courage to go against the grain of convention can buoy their companies to new heights while competitors are sinking.

Originally published in June 2001
Reprint R0106F

The Growth Crisis—
and How to Escape It

ADRIAN J. SLYWOTZKY AND RICHARD WISE

Executive Summary

AT A TIME WHEN COMPANIES are poised to seize the growth opportunities of a rebounding economy, many of them, whether they know it or not, face a growth crisis. Even during the boom years of the past decade, only a small fraction of companies enjoyed consistent double-digit revenue growth. And those that did often achieved it through short-term measures—such as mergers and inflated price increases—that don't provide the foundation for growth over the long term. But there is a way out of this predicament.

The authors claim that companies can achieve sustained growth by leveraging their "hidden assets," a wide array of underused, intangible capabilities and advantages that most established companies already hold. To date, much of the research on intangible assets has centered on intellectual property and brand recognition. But in this article, the authors uncover a host of other assets that can help spark growth. They identify four major categories of hidden assets: customer relationships, strategic real estate, networks, and information. And they illustrate each with an example of a company that has creatively used its hidden assets to produce new sources of revenue.

Executives have spent years learning to create growth using products, facilities, and working capital. But they should really focus on mobilizing their hidden assets to serve their customers' higher-order needs—in other words, create offerings that make customers' lives easier, better, or less expensive. Making that shift in mind-set isn't easy, admit the authors, but companies that do it may not only create meaningful new value for their customers but also produce double-digit revenue and earnings growth for investors.

Deep down, executives know that achieving strong and sustained top-line growth is getting tougher. They may be able to temporarily boost earnings by slashing costs. They may be able to inflate their companies' share prices with the promise of future profits. But steady sales gains remain elusive. Even during the boom years of the past decade, consistently strong revenue growth—the foundation of steady earnings and share price growth—was the exception: From 1990 to 2000, just 10% of publicly traded companies enjoyed eight or more years of double-digit growth in their top line.

To managers daunted by the challenge, we offer some bad news and some good news. First, the bad news: Things are even worse than they appear. Tactics used in recent years to increase revenue are running out of steam and will no longer provide the foundation for long-term, double-digit growth. Now for the good news: You are probably sitting on a solution to the problem. Sustained growth can be achieved by leveraging your company's hidden assets, a wide array of underutilized, intangible capabilities and advantages that most established companies already possess.

Many companies with apparently strong records of growth have achieved them through unsustainable moves.

Why, you may wonder, do we call such assets "hidden"? There has, after all, been much discussion of the increasing importance of intangibles. But the discussion to date has tended to focus on the valuation of intangible assets, a misguided and probably impossible task; what's more important is how you use these assets to drive new growth. Moreover, the discussion has typically been limited to such traditional intangibles as brands and intellectual property. But in fact, a much broader set of assets can be leveraged to produce growth. While some of them may appear familiar, the trick is in recognizing which ones can be deployed most effectively in your company and learning how to make that happen. Before we show you how to do that, let's examine why these assets have become so vitally important.

Stripping off the Growth Masks

The trend of lackluster revenue growth in recent years is disturbing, to be sure. But even more unsettling is the fact that many companies with apparently strong records of growth have achieved them through unsustainable, incremental moves—such as international expansion, acquisitions, or aggressive price increases—rather than through steady growth from the core business. When we accounted for such tactical measures in our analysis of major companies in numerous industries, we discovered that their core businesses were expanding at a relatively slow pace, and some were actually shrinking. (See the exhibit "Growth: Sluggish at the Core.") Let's look at these growth masks in more detail.

International markets, for example, are often viewed as a rich field for growth, but in reality they hold little opportunity for sustained gains in many industries. The largest of these markets, in Western Europe and Japan, are as competitive and mature as those in the United States. And emerging markets, despite the "billion consumers in China" rhetoric, are usually much smaller and are typically characterized by weak consumer and industrial purchasing power, inefficient distribution channels, economic instability, and protectionist laws. When an emerging market finally looks promising, it often produces competitors that challenge you not only in their home markets but also on your own turf. Just think of Korea's Samsung and Hyundai.

Mergers and acquisitions were a huge component of the 1990s growth story, as M&A activity grew sevenfold from 1994 to 1999, to $1.4 trillion. But the rapid pace of deal making is unlikely to continue. Investor enthusiasm for such moves has started to fade, as acquisitions rarely produce new value and often lead to disaster. Moreover, the inflated stock prices that allowed many companies to make cheap acquisitions in recent years have dropped back to more reasonable levels. And in many industries, consolidation has drastically reduced the number of

Growth: Sluggish at the Core

Many companies have relied on unsustainable tactics to paint a picture of enhanced revenue growth. Our analysis found that, after stripping away these growth marks, the largest companies (for which public data were available) in 11 major industries enjoyed only modest core growth—if they saw any at all.

Company	1995–2000 Overall compound annual revenue growth		International growth[1]		Acquisitions[2]		Price increases[3]		Estimated core growth
J.P. Morgan Chase	31.3%	–	9.4%	–	12.3%	–	4.5%	=	5.1%
Boeing	21.1%	–	4.8%	–	6.7%	–	1.7%	=	7.9%
Disney	15.9%	–	1.3%	–	6.3%	–	1.6%	=	6.7%
ExxonMobil	13.4%	–	6.9%	–	3.0%	–	10.5%	=	–7.0%
Alcoa	12.9%	–	2.0%	–	6.2%	+	1.0%	=	5.7%
Emerson Electric	9.2%	–	3.3%	–	2.5%	+	2.8%	=	6.2%
Georgia-Pacific	9.2%	–	0.7%	–	3.9%	–	4.7%	=	–0.1%
MetLife	7.9%	+	3.0%	–	5.4%	–	4.5%	=	1.0%
Gillette	6.5%	–	1.9%	–	3.3%	–	1.4%	=	–0.1%
Caterpillar	5.5%	–	2.3%	–	0.6%	–	1.7%	=	0.9%
Procter & Gamble	3.6%	–	1.5%	–	0.7%	–	1.4%	=	0.0%

1. This column measures the growth from base international revenues in 1995, along with any international acquisitions.
2. This column measures the net change in revenue caused by domestic acquisitions and divestitures.
3. This column measures the change in price of the underlying commodity or industry segment (as measured by the Consumer Price Index or the Product Price Index, as applicable).

Source: Company 10-Ks, annual reports, and U.S. Bureau of Labor Statistics.

viable acquisition targets, thus making antitrust concerns a barrier to future growth through M&As.

As for growth through price increases, what worked over the past decade in many industries can't be counted on in the future. Even though overall inflation was muted in the 1990s, many companies were able to raise prices for certain product categories (such as breakfast cereal), classes of customers (such as business travelers), and commodities that enjoyed cyclical pricing opportunities (such as oil). But in most industries, demand has slackened and competition has intensified, giving companies little room to push through reflexive price increases. Indeed, many businesses are now concentrating on minimizing price declines.

One mask that we didn't examine—and that is much harder to peel away—is the aggressive and sometimes dubious accounting practices that boost reported revenues. These artificial revenue enhancements, used in recent years by Enron and a host of other companies, include off-balance-sheet purchases and sales, revenue swaps, undisclosed acquisitions, quid pro quo sales linked to equity investments, and accelerated recognition of leasing and service contract revenue, among others. The prevalence of such practices is, at one level, a tacit acknowledgment of the growth crisis facing many companies today.

Looking for Growth in All the Wrong Places

Once you strip off the growth masks, you find widespread stagnation in many companies' core businesses. The hard truth is that most companies have started to run up against the limits of growth based on products alone, whether they are manufactured goods or the "products" of a service business.

That's because, for one thing, many markets are saturated. In most developed countries, consumers have all
the appliances, tires, and credit cards they need; businesses are awash in copiers, chemicals, and machinery.
In addition, the sheer number of products has exploded,
which has diced already saturated markets into ever-
smaller pieces. To give just one example, the number of
food product SKUs (stock-keeping units) in the United
States grew fivefold, to nearly 11,000, from 1980 to 1998,
according to the Federal Reserve Bank of Dallas. Thus,
even a company's own product extensions—think of
Vanilla Coke and Wild Cherry Pepsi—undermine efforts
to generate profitable new growth; they lead the company into increasingly tiny market niches while introducing higher marketing and distribution costs.

Another reason for the growth crisis is that innovation has slowed in many traditional industries, resulting
in products that are largely undifferentiated in performance. Think of Boeing and Airbus, Ford and General
Motors, John Deere and Caterpillar. In other industries,
back-and-forth jockeying occurs, as first one competitor
and then another introduces a product with slightly better performance. Think of Nintendo and Sony, Intel and
AMD. Product improvements aren't a source of long-
term growth for any of these companies.

Furthermore, in recent years, the development of
entirely new products has proven to be an unreliable
source of growth. Breakthrough innovation has continued in certain high-tech industries, to be sure. But even
there, sustained growth is rare. Our analysis of high-tech
leaders' stock performance over the past two decades
reveals a disturbing pattern: They experience a couple of
years of spectacular market value growth followed by
equally spectacular collapse. (See the exhibit "A Succes-
sion of Bottle Rockets.") Each company's stock circuit

A Succession of Bottle Rockets

New product innovation has proved to be a source of only fleeting growth over the past two decades. Even the leading technology companies have experienced what might be called bottle rocket trajectories: The period of time for them to climb from 50% of their peak market value to the apex and then tumble back again as revenue growth stalls has lasted just three to five years. Market data for each group represent an index of the companies' stock prices.

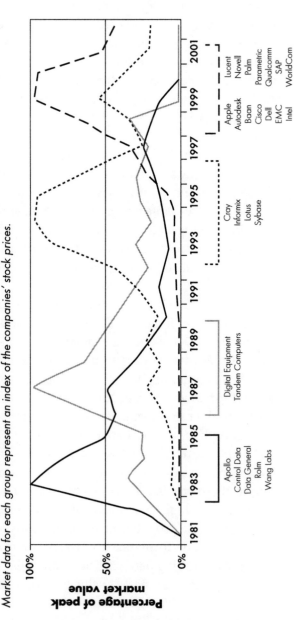

correlated with a rise and then stall in revenue, caused by the saturation of its product market, attacks by competitors, or a shift in customer priorities. The lesson: Businesses built around high-tech product innovation are dramatically unstable.

As a result of all these factors, most companies cannot offer investors a compelling vision of a ten-year run of robust growth. That's true not only for companies with a history of reported problems, such as Procter & Gamble, but also for companies that, until recently, were widely considered powerhouses, such as Merck and AOL Time Warner. Even strong companies such as Wal-Mart and Southwest Airlines will need to examine how much growth momentum they can maintain with their current strategies.

How does your company measure up? If you take a hard look at your core business, you will likely find that your growth rate has declined from double to single digits. (To diagnose your company's growth rate and identify the organizational challenges you face in improving it, see the work sheet "Determining Your Core Growth.") Your analysis may give you just enough time to head off the stall. After all, identifying and leveraging the resources needed to generate renewed growth can't be achieved overnight. Indeed, most executives have their hands full dealing with more immediate crises—in particular, the demands of analysts and investors clamoring for short-term performance enhancement.

Spotting Next-Generation Demand

So how can a company overcome the limits of product-centric growth? Managers willing to take a longer view of their company's performance can capitalize on assets

Determining Your Core Growth

Do you know what your company's true growth rate is? By plugging some hard data into this work sheet and making a few rough calculations, you'll be able to assess how your company measures up. No matter which challenge you currently face—be it owning up to your growth crisis or maintaining a robust rate of growth—asking some tough questions will help you improve your performance.

What is your core growth rate?

What is the current annual revenue of your company? a $ _____

What was the annual revenue five years ago? b $ _____

Estimate the domestic revenue of companies you acquired over the past
five years. c $ _____

Estimate the change in international revenue over the past five years. d $ _____

Estimate any revenue derived from creative changes in revenue recognition
policies over the past five years. * e $ _____

Estimate the average annual price increases for your products over the past
five years. f _____ %

Calculate an estimate of your core growth rate = $\{[(a-b-c-d-e)\div b]\div 5\}-f$ _____ %

If > 5%

If < 5%

Current crisis

Organizational challenge: Having the discipline to invest
in new growth while facing declining fortunes

Questions to ask:
- Which activities can we scale back to free resources for
growth initiatives?
- What is the right growth sequence to maximize short-
term gains while preserving long-term potential?

What is your relative performance?

How does your growth rate compare with:

your market value growth?

your earnings growth?

the core growth rate of your leading competitors?

Lagging	Comparable	Higher
Lagging	Comparable	Higher
Lagging	Comparable	Higher

If comparable or higher

If lagging

Are your growth prospects robust?

By what amount do you expect your market to grow over the next five years?

Multiply that by the percentage share you expect to capture.

$$\$ \underline{\quad} \times \frac{\%}{\underline{\quad}} = g\ \$ \underline{\quad}$$

How much new revenue is reasonably available through acquisition over the next five years?

$$h\ \$ \underline{\quad}$$

What is the potential for new revenue in international markets over the next five years?

$$i\ \$ \underline{\quad}$$

Calculate an estimate of your average annual growth rate = $[(g+h+i)\div 5]\div a$

$\underline{\quad}\%$

If < 5%

If > 5%

Impending problem

Organizational challenge: Moving quickly to avoid value collapse

Questions to ask:

• What is our process for identifying and exploiting growth opportunities?

• How do we need to change investors' views and expectations on the sources of future growth?

Looming stall

Organizational challenge: Forcing your company to focus on challenging growth moves in good times

Questions to ask:

• What growth moves are open to us if we move now instead of waiting?

• Where will customers' priorities lie three years from now?

Robust outlook

Organizational challenge: Backing up your growth vision by committing time, talent, and resources to it

Questions to ask:

• Have we funded our growth initiatives with resources commensurate with our expectations?

• Do we have the right talent and incentives in place to support new initiatives?

*These include policies such as accelerated recognition of service contract revenue, reclassification of onetime gains as revenue, revenue swaps, undisclosed acquisitions, channel stuffing, and quid pro quo sales linked to equity investments.

they already own to address what we call "higher-order needs." These unmet customer demands don't involve incremental improvements in product features and functionality. Rather, they reflect customers' need to improve their overall economics, in which the product plays just one role.

For example, an industrial products company might help customers improve their operating efficiency by offering maintenance support, remote monitoring, or complete operations outsourcing. It might help customers reduce their risk by offering insurance or output guarantees. Most industries harbor abundant opportunities to go beyond the product and address this next generation of demand.

Look at the largely stagnant automotive components business. In the 1990s, Johnson Controls shifted its focus from assembling automobile seats, a commodity product, to providing automakers with integrated interior modules and, more recently, complete cockpits. Thus, the company moved from simply manufacturing a high-quality product to addressing automakers' higher-order needs: reducing the risk and complexity of vehicle design and improving the efficiency of vehicle assembly.

Today, Johnson not only earns more revenue per vehicle but also reaps higher margins because the value it offers includes specialized design, consumer research, testing, and supplier management. As a result, Johnson has achieved double-digit growth in revenue, operating profits, and market value over the past decade, while most automotive suppliers have experienced slow growth and shrinking margins. Furthermore, by focusing on its customers' higher-order needs, Johnson has moved into a much larger market than its previous one: the $85 billion interiors market, rather than the $7 billion seat assembly market.

Business customers aren't the only ones with higher-order needs; consumers have them, too, although they are often less directly tied to dollars-and-cents economics. One is the need to improve the ease and efficiency with which products and services are purchased and consumed—what might be called time-and-hassle economics.

Consider Sears Great Indoors, a store that brings all of the major products and services involved in home remodeling under one roof. It offers consumers a single source for flooring, lighting, kitchen and bathroom fixtures, appliances, curtains, accent items, and furnishings. It combines this with a full spectrum of services for the entire project, from design and financing to construction and installation. Thus, Sears Great Indoors cuts shopping time, streamlines the project-planning process, and improves the quality of the finished work by ensuring that all the products chosen fit together physically and aesthetically. The positive impact on consumers' time-and-hassle economics is profound, while the new business gives Sears a strong position in the $150 billion home-remodeling market.

Established businesses have spent many years, thousands of staff hours, and billions of dollars building their hidden assets—the natural by-products of creating core products and services.

It's one thing, of course, to give customers new offerings that improve their economics; it's quite another to do so profitably enough to generate significant new value for your company. That's why it's crucial to ascertain that your assets are suited to addressing your customers' higher-order needs and that they can be used to meet those needs more profitably than competitors' assets.

Leveraging Your Hidden Assets

The challenge of maintaining growth often becomes greater the bigger a company gets. Fortunately, most established businesses have an array of underutilized resources they can leverage. Indeed, these companies have spent many years, thousands of staff hours, and billions of dollars building their hidden assets—the natural by-products of creating and delivering core products and services. Skillfully employed, they enable a company to produce a portfolio of related offerings, often with unusually high margins.

In the case of Johnson Controls, the hidden asset was the company's market position. Because it was a leading player in seating—the most valuable and complicated interior subsystem but one that was also relatively self-contained and thus could be outsourced—Johnson was uniquely positioned to take on the role of systems integrator. It could amortize its investments in new research and design skills more easily than smaller or peripheral players could. Sears's hidden assets were its unique authority with customers in home hard goods, such as kitchen appliances, and its skill at managing a network of independent contractors, developed through its long-standing Sears Home Services business.

The beauty of such assets is that, once created, they can be applied, reused, and extended at little or no marginal cost. What's more, new rivals will be hard-pressed to replicate your strategy. Start-ups will need to build from scratch the hidden assets that incumbents have developed at extraordinary expense, both in dollars and in hours of employee learning.

We're not saying that hidden assets alone are sufficient to address higher-order needs profitably. Most companies will have to enhance the power of their existing asset base through acquisitions, partnerships, or licensing. But while a combination of tangible assets, hidden assets, and acquired or licensed assets are needed to create a unique and profitable strategic position, owning the hidden assets can tip the balance in favor of a new business being both differentiated and profitable.

Hidden assets have at least two other benefits. First, using them to address customers' higher-order needs tends to reinforce, rather than cannibalize, the core product business on which they are based. By crafting a multidimensional connection with your customers, you're in a better position from which to sell your traditional products. Second, when you leverage your hidden assets, they frequently engender new assets that lead to yet more offerings. In other words, the more you use them, the more you have. Establishing additional touch points with your customers just gives you more opportunities to understand—and solve—their problems.

You can see that using hidden assets to meet higher-order customer needs provides a path to new growth that represents a hybrid between two traditional growth routes. This approach holds much more potential than the incremental growth typical of product and brand extensions. But it is much less risky than "white space" business moves—trying to develop new products for new markets—because it is built on the solid foundation of your existing products and customers.

An Array of Riches

The traditional intangible assets—intellectual property, competency in a particular area, brand recognition—are certainly important, but as we have seen, the universe of valuable intangible assets is much broader and richer. The exhibit "A Universe of Hidden Assets" lists 15 types of such assets, organized into four categories: customer relationships, strategic real estate, networks, and information. We will look in detail at one asset in each category.

CUSTOMER RELATIONSHIPS

Assets in this category provide a critical gateway to understanding and addressing higher-order needs. they allow you to deliver new offerings that are more sophisticated, less expensive to develop, and likely to be more readily accepted than your competitors'—typically at premium prices. Some companies have great *reach*. Others have a unique level of customer *interaction* or have *insight* into customers' business issues. One company that has developed an especially creative approach to leveraging its *authority* is John Deere.

This maker of high-end, tractor-style lawn mowers, as well as bigger agricultural equipment, owns a powerful brand name. But beyond brand recognition, the company has also developed a reputation for its expertise in lawn care among landscapers—contractors who not only design and install lawns and gardens but also maintain them. Because the lawn-care equipment market is highly cyclical and slow growing, Deere looked for ways to spark new growth.

The landscaping industry is highly fragmented, which means that landscapers must deal with multiple suppliers to procure the goods and services they need. John Deere realized that integrating the purchasing process and developing such services as consumer financing could significantly improve the landscapers' business economics. The company believed it could capitalize on its reputation: Customers would trust it to sell more than just lawn equipment.

First, though, John Deere needed to enhance this existing hidden asset with more traditional ones. So it purchased the two biggest companies in the nursery products and irrigation products industries. Their 200-plus outlets, renamed John Deere Landscapes, now provide one-stop shopping for both landscaping and sprinkler products, many branded with John Deere's leaping-deer logo. The Deere name has boosted sales and margins at the outlets. Satellite showrooms for lawn tractors and other equipment will be added at major locations, giving landscapers more opportunities to see and touch the company's latest machines as well as helping John Deere develop stronger customer relationships.

Finally, the company has begun offering ancillary services. Its credit program, for instance, lets landscapers offer financing of major projects to their homeowner customers. This type of service—typically beyond the financial reach of landscaping businesses, which tend to be small operations—helps landscapers build stronger ties with their own customers. And Deere benefits, too. Because most purchasers of high-end landscaping services are excellent credit risks, the business is solidly profitable.

The John Deere Landscapes business has greatly increased interactions between landscapers and John Deere dealers, bolstering yet another hidden asset. It has also moved the company beyond the mature $20 billion landscaping equipment market and into the much faster-growing and higher-margin $100 billion landscaping market. Although entering this market required

A Universe of Hidden Assets

Most companies know how to leverage traditional intangible assets such as brand, intellectual property, and competency in a particular area. But these represent only a fraction of the capabilities and advantages that companies have at their disposal.

Category	Asset type	Company with assets to exploit
Customer Relationships	*Reach:* Being able to touch a large number of customers	McDonald's serves 48 million customers a day.
	Interaction: Having frequent or meaningful contact with customers	Wal-Mart customers visit its Supercenters twice as often as they do traditional discount stores.
	Insight: Possessing detailed knowledge about customers and their business problems	GE Plastics has expertise in automobile-component design issues.
	Authority: Having the reputation as an expert in a given field	UPS is considered an expert in logistics.
	Value chain position: Occupying a position of advantage within the chain of suppliers, manufacturers, and consumers	Dell occupies a valuable space between computer manufacturers and end users.
Strategic Real Estate	*Market position:* Being in a strong position relative to competitors	DeWolfe Realty's role as a broker of homes allows it to seize follow-on mortgage and insurance sales.
Networks	*Portal:* Controlling a gateway that others must use to access information, products, or services	Gemstar–TV Guide International's interactive television-program guide serves 15 million homes.
	Third-party relationships: Having unique relationships with key partners such as suppliers or content producers	Oracle has a broad set of horizontal and vertical application-development partners.

Category	Asset type	Company with assets to exploit
	Installed base: Having access to owners and users of your product or service	Boeing has an installed base of more than 13,000 commercial jetliners, roughly 75% of the world fleet.
	User community: Having a set of people who consider themselves part of a larger group defined by its relationship to your product	Harley-Davidson has an active owners' group of 650,000 riders and enthusiasts.
	Deal flow: Receiving preferential access to potential transactions, typically M&A opportunities, within or adjacent to your industry	Cisco has early access to virtually every potential deal in the networking industry.
	Market window: Having superior vision into marketplace activity	Knight Trading sees movements in the equities industry because of its role as a market maker.
Information	*Technical know-how:* Possessing deep, often proprietary, technical knowledge in an area of importance to customers	IBM is an expert in SAP software implementation.
	Software and systems: Owning internally developed IT systems with potential external value	American Airlines has a robust in-house reservation management tool, which serves as the basis for Sabre, the leading flight reservation and booking system.
	By-product information: Possessing information gained through current business operations that has value outside the business in which it was generated	Quintiles Transnational generates drug usage information in its clinical-trial management business that is valuable to pharmaceutical marketing departments.

Deere to make a number of acquisitions, it required no additional investment in its relevant hidden asset: its authority with customers.

STRATEGIC REAL ESTATE

Assets in this category relate to the position a company occupies within its industry. That might be a particularly strong *market position* or control of a *portal* through which others must pass to access information, products, or services. Such assets allow a company to enter new markets more quickly and more cheaply than competitors can. Consider how the pharmaceutical distributor Cardinal Health leveraged its *value chain position* to capitalize on the expertise, systems, and information gained in its once-restrictive middleman role.

Eight years ago, Cardinal Health was one of several large players in a notoriously low-margin business: It essentially delivered pills from Point A to Point B. But the company was strategically positioned at the heart of the pharmaceutical value chain, which linked it with 26,000 retail pharmacies, hospital groups, managed care providers, and pharmaceutical manufacturers. Cardinal's unique vantage point gave it powerful insights into the rapidly changing pharmaceutical marketplace, and its executives realized that the company could create offerings that would meet the needs of both its customers and suppliers.

Downstream, hospitals and independent pharmacies were experiencing growing cost pressures while trying to maintain quality care. They also faced other challenges, including the management of an increasingly complex body of patient and financial information. To address these problems, Cardinal developed a series of businesses

leveraging its position in the value chain. Using its distribution experience in inventory management and pro-
curement, Cardinal began to host information systems
for hospital pharmacies. It developed automated technology for ordering and dispensing medications and dis-
tributing them to hospital patients, thereby reducing loss
and theft, improving accuracy, and maximizing data capture. That, in turn, led to the development of a range of
hospital pharmacy management services, from staffing to
consulting to complete outsourcing of the pharmaceutical function. Cardinal also introduced a franchise option
to independent retail pharmacists, offering them information systems, marketing resources, and purchasing
power that were once beyond their reach.

Upstream, Cardinal created specialized services for
drug makers. These services—in which Cardinal would
design and produce customized packaging for drugs—
again leveraged the intimate market knowledge it
derived from its central position in the value chain. The
company reduced its overall manufacturing and distribution costs by linking the two functions, which enabled
just-in-time replenishment and smaller inventories. Cardinal was able to aggregate demand for less common
dosage forms, such as freeze-dried tablets, from multiple
pharmaceutical companies to achieve scale production
advantages. And it was able to profitably meet hospitals'
needs for custom packaging of certain drugs—something most pharmaceutical companies, with their siloed
manufacturing operations, did poorly, if at all.

These strategic moves in both directions on the
value chain let Cardinal expand its economic horizons
beyond the pharmaceutical distribution market. Now
it's a major player in a dramatically larger market—one
that encompasses consulting, information technology,

drug-packaging design and manufacture, pharmacy management, and other health care services. Today, Cardinal Health manages more pharmacies than all its competitors put together.

It handles prescription benefits for nearly 3 million individuals and provides automated drug deliveries to 4 million patients a day. These new businesses have generated a huge revenue stream with profit margins far greater than those in Cardinal's core business, but they also bolster the core business and give Cardinal the best distribution margins in the industry. Over the past decade, Cardinal's revenues, operating profits, and market value grew at double-digit rates, far outpacing its closest competitor.

NETWORKS

These hidden assets are based on a company's extended set of enterprise relationships. Having *third-party relationships* with suppliers or channels, for instance, or having a strong *user community* that shares information and experiences can be good sources for new offerings. Having access to a *deal flow*—that is, knowing about upcoming potential mergers—is another hidden asset. So is a company's *installed base* of products. Typically, the number of a company's products in use is much larger than its annual unit sales volume. And each of those products provides an opportunity for the company to offer maintenance, financing, insurance, operations assistance, and other potentially lucrative services.

Take General Motors. Most automakers don't consider their installed base to be a valuable asset. They have relatively few opportunities to interact with car owners, and when they do, the interactions are usually indirect (through independent dealerships) or under less-than-happy circumstances (when repairs are needed or a vehicle is recalled). GM's installed base totals more than 80 million vehicles and grows by 5 million annually. That gives GM countless opportunities to maintain a customer relationship or create a recurring revenue stream. Now, with its OnStar business, the company is moving to take advantage of this huge hidden asset.

The OnStar system offers a collection of in-vehicle services for the driver, including one-button access to route-planning information; notification to a central information center when a vehicle's airbag is deployed; remote unlocking capabilities; remote engine diagnostics monitoring; access to customized financial, traffic, and other information; and even concierge services.

OnStar improves the economics of using a car by reducing many of the hassles associated with driving. And it opens up growth opportunities for GM by creating recurring revenue streams in the form of monthly subscriptions, which will mount substantially as OnStar adds more services. For example, customers are now able to buy cellular telephone airtime and satellite-based digital radio service through OnStar. To offer such services, GM formed partnerships with numerous companies that provide voice recognition technology, cellular phone hardware, and digital radio service.

But the primary asset GM leveraged in creating OnStar was its ever-growing installed base, which gives it several significant competitive advantages. First, it gave GM distribution, system deployment, and customer acquisition advantages over rivals because OnStar's hardware can be installed, marketed, and financed as part of GM's traditional vehicle options packages. In fact, OnStar has a 70% cost advantage over an equivalent service that requires installation after the car is purchased. In addition, the unequaled size of GM's installed base means that the company's service will likely become a de facto standard, attracting the best new applications and content developers and creating network advantages for users of the system. OnStar is now available in Acura, Lexus, Audi, and Subaru vehicles, giving it an installed base that extends beyond its own automobiles.

OnStar already has more than 2 million subscribers, each of whom now has a direct connection to GM instead of an indirect one through the dealer. As OnStar adds services and enhances existing ones, GM's core business will benefit: A growing number of GM car buyers will have an ongoing relationship with the company once they drive off the dealer's lot, and GM will gain more information and insight into their behavior.

INFORMATION

Hidden assets in this category are among the most underutilized. Although companies have made huge investments in software, systems, and infrastructure to capture and manipulate information about their businesses over the past decade, few companies have used these investments to serve customers' higher-order needs and create new growth.

Information assets are well suited to this task. They can help manage risk, streamline workflows, improve decision making, and anticipate problems. Moreover, although information systems are expensive and time-consuming to build, once the software has been written and the information has been captured, they can be reused at very low marginal cost.

These assets include an advantaged *market window* into the activity of a particular industry, proprietary *technical know-how,* and internally developed *software and systems* that may have external value. Hanover Compressor, originally a gas-equipment rental company, made use of *by-product information* to offer customers an unusual service.

Hanover once simply rented out its equipment, which is used to move natural gas through production and distribution pipelines. Recently, however, the company has redefined its business, applying its unique information assets and making a series of supporting acquisitions to satisfy various levels of its customers' higher-order needs.

Hanover began its transition by leveraging another hidden asset: its repeated interactions with customers as compression requirements changed over the life of a gas well. Through these interactions, Hanover gained a clearer picture of customer needs. As a result, it expanded its offerings of gas production equipment and services; for instance, it took over the management and maintenance of customers' pipeline-monitoring systems. To deploy that service economically, it developed remote-monitoring technology that provides a real-time picture of its customers' production systems, capturing a wealth of data about pipeline flows, gas impurities, processing downtimes, and other industry metrics.

Building on this flow of data, created as a by-product of effectively managing its monitoring business, Hanover now offers services that address its customers' ultimate higher-order needs: cost predictability and risk minimization. Leveraging its by-product information, Hanover offers performance guarantees that cover both the quality and quantity of gas flowing through its customers' pipelines. Note that the asset Hanover exploited, by-product information, actually grew out of its exploitation of another asset: its numerous interactions with customers. That's a perfect example of the way in which hidden assets tend to multiply.

Hanover's new offerings expand the company's potential market sixfold. Rather than simply monitor customers' activities, Hanover is a crucial participant in them. Meanwhile, its market share in its core compressor business has risen from 20% to 40%. That's partly the result of acquisitions, but it is also the result of the skillful deployment of the company's hidden assets. Indeed, over the past decade, Hanover has generated double-digit growth in revenues, operating profits, and market growth.

Companies in other industries are beginning to make similar information-based moves, using assets that have sprung from their deployment of other hidden assets. For example, Cardinal Health has recently created a venture to package and sell real-time information about wholesale and retail drug sales to pharmaceutical marketers. The business is a valuable by-product of its distribution and pharmacy management services. Today's nascent information-based businesses represent only the early stages of a new source of growth, as scores of incumbent companies begin to leverage the information assets they've built over the years.

Several trends are likely to drive information-based growth in the near future. Investment in information technology will continue to grow over the long term. And the digitization of analog information—from X-ray images to movies—will increase the flexibility and value of information-based offerings. Furthermore, the spread of embedded intelligence and pervasive networks means that information can increasingly reach customers almost anywhere.

Changing Your Mind-Set

Learning to mobilize your hidden assets to serve your customers' higher-order needs is not easy. Most executives have spent years learning to create growth using products, factories, facilities, and working capital. They have spent much less time thinking about how to use a combination of relationships, market position, networks, and information—their hidden assets—to create value for customers and growth for investors.

Managers must learn this critical skill if they hope to generate large-scale, long-term growth. The experiences of several companies in tough industries—companies such as John Deere, Cardinal Health, General Motors, and Hanover Compressor—show that doing so can be extremely rewarding.

Most businesses will face significant organizational barriers to making the change. But the first step lies with the individual executive, who must acknowledge the limits of traditional product-centric growth, rethink the nature of demand, and then creatively identify and manage previously underutilized assets to profitably satisfy customers' needs. This shift in mind-set—at the individual or the organizational level—won't happen overnight. But companies that make the shift will be well positioned to create meaningful new value for customers and double-digit revenue and earnings growth for investors.

Originally published in July 2002
Reprint R0207E

After the Layoffs, What Next?

SUZY WETLAUFER

Executive Summary

HARRY DENTON, THE CEO in this fictional case study, has been caught off guard. As the head of Delarks, a venerable department-store chain in the Midwest, he has engineered a remarkable turnaround in only a year. Sales have rebounded, and Wall Street is applauding. Sure, a few trees were felled in the process—to make room for new growth, Denton had to clear out 3,000 pieces of what he privately refers to as "deadwood"—but he'd saved the company. Didn't people understand that?

Not exactly. When Delarks's head of merchandising defects to a competitor, Denton is shocked to realize that many of the survivors, in fact, have had it with him and with the company. The last straw was the recent closing of the Madison store, which Denton announced without warning to anyone—not even the company's head of HR, Thomas Wazinsky, a supposedly trusted adviser. In the

49

wake of that coup, store employees from Wichita to Peoria are wondering, Are we next? The rumor mill says that many of them are considering leaving before Denton can inflict the next blow. And senior managers are not immune to the fear and anger. Even Wazinsky, one of the few links to Delarks's proud past, confesses to Denton, "I'll bet you're thinking of firing me."

Denton has to act—and fast. He calls a "town meeting" for the 600 employees of the St. Paul store. The plan: rally the troops. Instead, Denton is routed. Angry questions are hurled at the CEO, and he is forced to beat a hasty retreat through the back door.

Five experts offer advice on how to revive morale at the successful but troubled company.

"**P**ERIWINKLE, DEFINITELY periwinkle." Claire Ladd's insistent voice filled the room, but it was greeted with dead silence.

"Did you hear me, Harry? I said *periwinkle*. It's *the* color of the fall season. And Harry, no suits this year. We're seeing all separates out of Milan, Paris, and Seventh Avenue. The woman's suit is dead."

Harry Denton shook his head and stared blankly at the woman across his desk. He knew he should be paying attention to her. After all, Claire Ladd represented a major apparel distributor for Delarks, the Chicago-based department-store chain of which he was CEO. But ever since Denton had read that morning's *Women's Wear Daily*, he had been unable to concentrate on anything but the headline stripped across the top of the second page: "Delarks Merchandising Chief Defects—Will Others Follow?"

Ladd walked around Denton's desk and gently shook him by the shoulders. In the 20-odd years they had known each other, starting when they were both "rack runners" in New York's bustling garment district, their relationship had always been honest—and even familial. "Snap out of it, Harry!" she laughed. "I'm not hawking periwinkle sweater sets for my health. Are we going to place orders here today or not?" When there was no immediate response, Ladd leaned closer, looking at Denton quizzically. "I mean, Harry," she said, "I was expecting a big order from you—everyone says Delarks is soaring again. You saved the chain. You're a hero on Wall Street. And when I was walking through the Springfield store last week, the place was filled with customers. It was packed—not like the old days, when you could set off a cannon in there and no one would notice. And Harry, the customers: they were *buying*. We like that."

Denton sighed. He liked it too. In fact, he loved it, as did the company's board of directors. Just that Monday, they had informed him that his contract had been renewed for two more years, with an increased salary and more stock options. They were delighted with his performance—and with Delarks. In just one year, Denton had transformed Delarks from a boring, outdated chain that catered to "aging dowager princesses," as Denton called them, into a fun, chic shopping emporium for the Midwest's growing population of affluent female baby boomers. The 28-store chain, with shops in small and midsize cities such as Bismarck, North Dakota, and Peoria, Illinois, had been on the verge of bankruptcy when Harry was lured away from his job

> *The problem, Denton knew, was that Delarks's transformation had involved quite a bit of bloodshed.*

running a national chain's flagship store in Manhattan. Now Delarks's success was the talk of the retail industry, in large part due to a leap in revenues to $400 million and the accompanying 20% surge in the chain's stock price. But the truth was, success wasn't tasting as sweet as Denton had hoped it would.

The problem, Denton knew, was that Delarks's transformation had involved quite a bit of bloodshed in the form of layoffs. Turnarounds always do; Denton had made that clear to his direct reports in his first week on the job. His strategy included refurbishing dowdy-looking stores and slashing overhead to meet the huge remodeling costs. And the strategy emphasized the need for a highly trained sales force that could execute "link selling," in which shoppers who enter the store looking for one product end up leaving with five, and feeling happy about it to boot. Link selling meant that "dead-wood"—a term he never used publicly, of course—would have to be cleared out to make room for a new breed of sophisticated, energized sales associates.

In other words, Denton told himself, layoffs had been inevitable. Especially at a company like Delarks, which had for years been run by an old-fashioned, even patriar-chal, group of managers led by the founder's son. Even after Delarks went public in 1988 and hired some new senior managers, the chain boasted salaries and benefits that were out of line for the industry, as well as a no-layoff policy.

Denton was well aware of that policy when he made the decision to cut Delarks's employment rolls by 20%, about 3,000 people in all. Some of the layoffs were less painful than others. For instance, most people under-stood that the chain's in-store restaurants had to be shut down. Gone were the days when women had time for a leisurely lunch as they shopped. The restaurants were rarely busy; closing them eliminated about 400 jobs. The consolidation of several half-empty distribution centers was also widely accepted by the organization. But people seemed to take the firing of several hundred longtime saleswomen very hard. Denton had predicted such a reaction, but he knew he had no choice: many of the old-timers were the lowest producers. And they had

The survivors were angry. Many thought Denton should have held meetings before the layoffs to warn people they were coming.

neither the abilities required for link selling nor a feel for the new kind of merchandise Delarks was offering: urban, modern, and trendy.

The pink slips had gone out on a Friday morning before lunch. That was the way Denton had always done it; indeed, it was the way he had always seen it done in the industry. It gave people time to clean out their desks and say their good-byes before the end of the day. It also gave the survivors a weekend to cool off before returning to work. Denton wasn't cold-hearted about the process, but having lived through about a dozen

Denton's view was that when a company is in financial trouble and a new CEO is brought in, everyone knows that layoffs are next.

downsizings in his career, he believed there was really no "kinder, gentler" way to fire people. The best approach was to do it quickly and in one fell swoop, and to make sure that everyone received a fair severance package. In fact, Denton believed he had gone beyond fair. The laid-off employees had been given two months pay and free outplacement services for one month, practically an unheard-of deal in the retail industry.

Still, the reaction had been severe. Not so much from the fired people; most of them went quietly. But the survivors were angry, and even the new staff Denton had brought in with him were upset. Many thought he should have held meetings before the layoffs to warn people they were coming. But he had rejected that idea. His view was that when a company is in deep financial trouble and a new CEO is brought in to save it, everyone knows that layoffs are next. Why make matters worse by rubbing their noses in it?

But now Denton was nervous. The wounds opened by the layoffs were not healing. In the newspaper article about Rachel Meyer's defection, the reporter had speculated that the move by Delarks's head of merchandising was connected to the downsizing initiative. The company was a morass of bad feelings, the article suggested, although Meyer had said "no comment" when asked directly about morale at the company.

An anonymous source quoted in the article had been more forthcoming. "There's no trust at Delarks," the source had said. "People feel like senior management isn't honest with its people. They just want to fix up the company fast and mop up the damage later." Denton felt stung. Who had said that? Was it someone from inside? Denton felt he *had* been honest, although maybe in the rush of executing the turnaround he hadn't done enough to prove it.

"This company is a mess, Claire," Denton blurted out. "I feel like everything I've built in the last year is collapsing around me."

"What—you've got to be kidding!"

Denton pulled the newspaper out of his desk drawer and showed it to her. "Rachel Meyer is leaving," he said, "and she's walking right across the street to Blake and Company. That's bad on its own, but what if she takes other people with her? What if she takes Liz Garcia?"

Ladd frowned. Garcia was Delarks's director of sales-associate training and one of the main reasons for the chain's turnaround. Denton had brought her with him from New York, and she had performed just as expected, giving Delarks's sales associates the savvy, direction, and skills they needed to connect with the company's new clientele. Her contribution was critical, especially because Denton had switched the salespeople's compensation system from one based on salary to one based on commission.

"You can't lose Liz," Ladd said quietly. "Harry, I'm going to get out of here so you can take care of the business that really matters now. Can we meet in a week?"

Denton nodded. "Thanks, Claire," he said. "Maybe I'll have stopped the bleeding by then."

But by the next day, the bleeding was worse. Garcia was still on board. But Thomas Wazinsky, Delarks's head of HR, told Denton that rumors were flying: four or five other senior people were supposedly on their way out, including the head of the profitable store in Wichita, Kansas. And there was also talk that "legions" of salespeople were packing up to leave the company.

"Is this just talk?" Denton pressed Wazinsky. "Have you received any official resignations?"

"No—no letters," Wazinsky allowed. "But Harry, you've got to realize, people are terribly unhappy. Morale is really low."

"That's not what you told me when we paid $20,000 for that employee attitude survey!" Denton snapped. "It didn't say people were ready to quit in droves." Three months earlier, Wazinsky had hired a small, local consulting firm to take the pulse of the company's employees. The results showed that pockets of employees were disaffected but that most were satisfied with the chain's new strategy. The consulting firm said that the results were typical for a company going through a downsizing, and even a bit more positive than usual. But it also recommended that Denton get out into the organization soon, both to reassure people that there would be no more layoffs and to explain the ones that had been necessary.

Denton had taken part of the advice. He did visit about half of the stores, and he did explain why Delarks had laid people off, but he refused to promise that there would be no more layoffs. In a turnaround situation, Denton knew, you have to leave your options open. And in fact, Denton had been right not to make assurances. Four weeks after his visits to the field, he decided to shut the chain's worst-performing store, in Madison, Wisconsin, eliminating another 200 jobs. After that, Denton felt relatively sure that the downsizing of Delarks was over, but again, he thought it would be unwise to make that news public. Too risky.

Now Denton was reconsidering: the time may have come to tell people that no more layoffs were impending. He tried the idea out on Wazinsky.

"I doubt people will believe you," he replied. Wazinsky was one of the few executives left over from the old regime. A native of Minnesota, he had been with the chain nearly 30 years, his entire career. Denton felt as though Wazinsky had never warmed to him and at times had even wondered if he should let him go. But he had decided a few months ago that Wazinsky, on balance, was a very valuable resource: he was keyed in to the organization in a way that Denton was not. It sometimes seemed, in fact, as if Wazinsky knew every single employee in the company on a first-name basis.

"Harry, can I be straight with you?" Wazinsky asked.

"Of course. Aren't you always?"

Wazinsky shrugged. "I might as well go for broke here, since I think my days are numbered—"

"Are you quitting?" Harry cut him off.

"No," Wazinsky said, "but I bet you're thinking of firing me."

An awkward silence filled the CEO's office.

"You're not going to be fired, I promise you that," Denton said finally. He meant it, and as he said the words, he was struck by how much trouble he was in if even Wazinsky didn't trust him. After all, the two of them spoke every day, often about the most confidential details of the turnaround strategy. The one exception had been the closing of the Madison store. Denton hadn't told anyone about that in advance except for members of the board, for fear of the news leaking to the press before the employees heard officially.

"I guess I should have told you beforehand about Madison," Denton acknowledged.

"Madison was a big screwup, if you don't mind my saying," Wazinsky replied with a rueful smile. "Yes, you should have told me—and you should have told Sylvia O'Donnell, the store manager. She should *not* have gotten her letter along with everyone else. People aren't going to forget that." Wazinsky paused, then went on. "I mean, Harry, there are stories going all around this company about the day Madison closed. They say people ran

into Sylvia's office after the announcement and found
her sitting there in shock, shaking her head and saying, 'I
had no idea,' over and over again."

"I was just trying to make sure people didn't find out
through the press or the grapevine," Denton quietly
protested.

"Well, whatever you were trying to do doesn't matter
now," said Wazinsky. "It backfired."

"So now what?" Denton asked with a short laugh. "I
mean, it's crazy, isn't it? Sales are up, and I just got our
last quarter's results a few days ago. We're going to have
solid profits by year's end. But if the rumors are true, our
great big success is going to shrink in a hurry."

The two men stared at each other, lost in thought.
Then both started to talk at once. They were struck by
the same plan: to hold a series of "town meetings" at
every store in the chain, in which Denton would talk
straight with the employees. He would promise no more
layoffs, apologize for the ways those in the past had been
handled, and set the tone for the company's future. "We
need to clear the air," Denton said. "People should be cel-
ebrating around here, not complaining."

The first town meeting was called for two days later in
one of the chain's largest stores, in St. Paul, Minnesota.
All 600 employees were invited to attend the session,
which was held in the conference room of a hotel in
downtown St. Paul, near the store. As he surveyed the
crowd before going on stage, it looked to Denton as if all
600 employees were there. He couldn't help but notice
that the room was remarkably quiet. There was tension
in the air.

Denton was tense, too. At the airport in Chicago earlier that day, Wazinsky had approached him with a
pained look. "Harry, I just listened to a voice mail from

Liz," he said. "She wants to meet with you as soon as possible."

"How bad is it?" Denton demanded. "Is she leaving?"

"Well, she says she can't stand working in a place where everyone hates coming to work. My guess is she's considering joining Rachel across the street."

Now, several hours later, Denton tried to block out his concerns about Liz and summon up his confidence. He cleared his throat and began speaking. "Delarks is a retail chain to be proud of again," he said, "thanks to you. In the past 18 months, there have been many changes in the way Delarks does business. What we asked of you wasn't easy—far from it—but you rose to the challenge and made success happen."

"I'll be honest with you. I probably should have handled the downsizing differently—" Denton was cut off by raucous applause.

Denton had expected applause at that line, but there wasn't any. He moved on to the hard part: the layoffs. "I'll be honest with you," he began, "I probably should have handled the downsizing differently—"

Here, he *was* cut off by applause, raucous and prolonged. He waited until it died down, and continued. "Layoffs are never easy. I'm not even sure there is a 'right' way to do them. But I take full responsibility for doing them in a way that felt wrong to a lot of you."

Again, the room broke into loud applause. But Denton could tell the applause wasn't a positive release of energy: people looked angry. He decided to cut his losses and move right into the question and answer period.

He didn't recognize the first person to approach the microphone—a middle-aged man in a plaid flannel shirt. Denton figured he was someone from the stockroom.

"Delarks may be making a lot of money now, Mr. Denton," he said pointedly, "but it's not a family anymore. It doesn't feel right. You and your folks from New York are always hiding up there on the eighteenth floor. You don't care anything about the people who are earning your big salaries for you."

"You just fired people like Mae Collier without any warning. You broke the heart of the store that day."

Again, cheers.

The man continued, "You just fired people like Mae Collier without any warning. Just up and fired her. That woman gave her whole life to Delarks. She was like a mother to a lot of us, especially the girls on the sales floor. You treated her like a hired hand. That's not right. You broke the heart of the store that day."

Denton had no idea who Mae Collier was, and the truth probably showed on his face. She had been a saleswoman, obviously, and most likely one who had low sales per square foot. But beyond that . . .

"Is Mae coming back?" the man at the microphone interrupted Denton's thoughts.

Denton hadn't expected this. He knew he would have to handle tough questions about how he had managed the downsizing. He had even expected that he would have to grovel about how he had botched the Madison closing. But to be questioned about an individual employee like this Mae Collier—that was not something he had prepared for.

He stalled for a moment, but he knew there was no point trying to placate the crowd with some sort of fudged half-truth. When he spoke, his answer was simple. "No," he said, "Mae Collier is not coming back. None of the employees who were let go are coming back.

Delarks is a different store now, and we need to let go of the past and focus on the future, and our future is very bright."

Another member of the audience pushed her way to the microphone. "People are *hurting*, Mr. Denton," she almost shouted. "You can't talk about the future with us until you make up for the past."

"That's what I'm trying to do right now," he shot back, exasperated. "What do you think I'm standing up here for?"

No one answered directly, but the crowd was rumbling unhappily. Denton was about to speak again when Wazinsky appeared at his shoulder and pulled him back from the podium. "Don't dig yourself in any deeper," he whispered. "Wrap it up. Say you're sorry and let's get out of here."

Denton turned back to the crowd, ready to close the meeting with an appeal: give me chance, he wanted to say. But, looking out, he could see people were already filing toward the door. No one would listen to him anyway. He shut off his microphone and followed Wazinsky to a back exit of the hotel.

What should Delarks do to repair the damage caused by a mismanaged downsizing?

Five experts offer advice on how to revive morale at the successful but troubled company.

BOB PEIXOTTO *is president for total quality and human resources at L.L. Bean in Freeport, Maine.*

Harry Denton is increasingly isolated from the company he has chosen to lead. He has put strategy *before* people, when his people should have been an integral part of the strategy. In his quest for a bold turnaround, he has broken trust at every turn. Thomas Wazinsky speaks for the entire company when he confides, "I think my days are numbered. I bet you're thinking of firing me." Faced with fear and distrust and the imminent defections of top-level people, Denton needs to do the following:

Stabilize Key People

He must carefully assess his senior staff, deciding how much he trusts each person and determining the value that each brings to the company. Then he should sit down with them privately and acknowledge his mistakes and what he has learned. He should express his confidence in them, his desire to have each person on his team, and his vision for Delarks's future—including what's in it for them. Finally, he should ask for each person's commitment. Straight talk, heartfelt expressions of confidence, and a picture of an engaging future are more powerful motivators than any retention bonus.

Appoint a "Change Cosponsor"

Delarks has undergone a drastic restructuring. A CEO can rarely lead a change of such magnitude alone. Denton needs help. He should ask Wazinsky to cosponsor the company's change efforts.

As one of the few executives remaining from the old regime, Wazinsky seems to have unique credibility with the company's employees. If he is seen embracing the changes at Delarks, the whole effort will be viewed in a new light by the frontline people. But Denton will first have to heal the breach in trust that he opened up when he failed to tell Wazinsky about his plan to close the Madison store.

Clarify the Change Message

Although the downsizing is over with, Denton and his senior team need to develop a brief, compelling message that includes three elements: the case for change, a view of the future, and a commitment to what will not change. Everyone in the management team should know the message well and repeat it often.

The people at Delarks need to understand the case for change: how the industry changed and why the company needed to respond. Denton may want to go beyond the message, in fact, to launch an education program that would enrich people's understanding of the business, demonstrate commitment to their development, and show trust by sharing information. By creating business-savvy employees, the program would also make future efforts to change easier.

The view of the future should describe the key elements of the change: the refurbishment of stores, the repositioning of the product line, link selling, and the new compensation system for sales associates. It should make clear the desired outcome of the changes, and it must be based on values that the people at Delarks can embrace.

Finally, Denton needs to spend some time alone thinking about what will not change. He's already rejected Delarks's former customers as "aging dowager princesses" and its longtime employees as "deadwood." One can bet that these "private" confidences have spread widely enough to become legendary. Denton needs to find something about Delarks's past that he can personally appreciate and publicly revere, something he can use as a cornerstone for the company's future. Delarks's people need to know that Denton values their past efforts.

Communicate, Communicate, Communicate

Communication must be constant, candid, and two-way. Denton has been assuming that people understand his intentions. But, because of the company's longstanding policy against layoffs, they were not anticipating the downsizing. And many may not have recognized the company's deep financial troubles or the way the marketplace was changing. A 20% surge in the stock price has not been nearly as important to people deep in the organization as the trust, long-term relationships, and predictability that used to exist. Denton needs to develop listening posts to stay in touch with his organization. At L.L. Bean, for example, we sample reactions to potential changes from a specially selected panel of employees.

Denton should also resume the town meetings. In 1995, following a voluntary reduction in the workforce at Bean, company president Leon Gorman conducted 27 town meetings over a two-week period. Nearly a third of each meeting was reserved for questions from the audience. This was the richest part of each meeting. It let frontline people vent their feelings and know that they had been heard.

Invest in the Survivors

Delarks must create a way to help the sales force change. New performance expectations need to be clear and linked to the business case. The company has a golden opportunity to signal real trust in its frontline people by asking them to help define the competencies required for link selling. Top employees can be tapped as trainer-coaches to help their peers. Denton is likely to be surprised by the emergence of a group of energized leaders of change.

Drive Out Fear and Build in Trust

Denton should remove as much uncertainty as possible by declaring layoffs a last resort and by being clear about how decisions affecting individuals and stores will be made. People should understand that layoffs are not random acts and that their strong performance and support for the company's new directions can limit their vulnerability.

At the same time, it doesn't make strategic sense for Denton to assure people that there will never again be layoffs. No one would believe him. The only promises the company's leaders should be making are short-term tangible ones that can be kept.

Keep the Spirit of Change Alive

Communication should not be limited to a onetime town-meeting blitz. Delarks's leaders need to repeat frequently the key points about the change effort. Frontline people need continual opportunities to vent their feelings. New information about the company's direction should be delivered to employees regularly. Such updates can occur at team meetings and should focus on measurable goals and clear milestones; and questions should be welcome. As progress, small wins, and new behaviors are celebrated, a renewed sense of energy and momentum will carry Delarks to higher levels of prosperity.

JIM EMSHOFF *is CEO of IndeCap Enterprises, a consulting firm based in Lake Forest, Illinois.*

I'm surprised that Denton has been so successful in improving Delarks's performance. Generally, a company whose staff is unraveling wouldn't experience this kind of turnaround.

That does not mean I think Denton is some sort of miracle manager. To restore his employees' trust and rebuild morale, he has serious work to do. But let me be very clear about what he should *not* do: under no circumstances should Denton backpedal or pretend to "start over" with his current staff. He should definitely not hold another town meeting or any other event in which Delarks's employees are encouraged to rehash the bloodletting they have just lived through.

Why not? Because whether or not any of the employees realize it, they have all been through the toughest part of the restructuring. Denton has already convinced the employees, old and new, that if Delarks hadn't changed, it would be bankrupt. That's why he has a shiny new sales force in place. That's why he has successfully changed the merchandise and the way the stores are operated. And that's why, in an amazingly short time, Wall Street is taking notice. Saying to employees, "Trust me—when we get through this, we're going to have a stronger company," is difficult. Many senior managers fail to get this point across in turnarounds. Denton, somehow, has succeeded.

No, this is not the time to look back. Instead, Denton must begin to capitalize, in a very tangible way, on the solid foundation he has built. Specifically, he should focus on three things.

First, Capitalize on the Company's Financial Strength

The company's stock price—and its sales—are up. The stock may be rising on the early part of an S curve; it may shoot up even more rapidly in the near future. Denton needs to share that success with his senior management team by giving them a large stock-option award, phased in over five years. He needs to make sure that they have an incentive to remain with the company through thick and thin.

He should also open up an option or stock-grant program for all Delarks employees. People need to understand that the changes at Delarks are not just skin deep—that the company is no longer the old-school, paternalistic place it once was. And the way to do that is to let them into the organization's heart. Denton should want his employees to understand exactly what the restructuring was all about; he should want them to be looking at the

You can't work as a loner when you hold the top job in any organization.

financial pages in their newspapers and doing the math. The sales staff, the stock clerks, and the sanitary workers should see how a stock uptick means they will have that much more money for their retirement or for their children's college tuitions.

The sales associates need particular attention. If the commission program was designed properly, they should be taking in much more money than they did under Delarks's salary system. But Denton must make sure that the salespeople are drawing the right conclusions. They should understand that the commission program is a real, positive change resulting from the restructuring.

Second, Rebuild a Cohesive Senior Management Team

Build, in fact, might be a better term; it's not clear that Denton ever had a proper leadership team to begin with.

Denton is a loner, that much is certain. His way of keeping people in the dark has been largely responsible for all the free-floating anxiety in the organization. The fact is, you can't work as a loner when you hold the top job in any organization. This seems to be Denton's first leadership position, and anyone in a new job needs time to learn and adjust. Even so, Denton must change the way he manages.

He should start by focusing on Liz Garcia. After all, she came with him to this company. She had faith in him at some point—enough to leave another job—and she has been successful at Delarks. Denton should bring her in and say, "Look, we've crossed phase one of this thing, now the fun can begin. I want you to take the lead in building the next-generation plan for the sales associates. I'm making you responsible for tweaking the commission program to encourage cooperation among the salespeople. I'm here to help, and so is Wazinsky." And Denton should ask her some challenging questions. Can we rehire some of the old sales associates and retrain them in the new system? Do you think virtually all the stores' customers are new? Should the company segment its sales force? Have we missed other opportunities to turn the staff into a team? These assignments should remotivate Garcia. What she needs is an opportunity to move from being a trainer to becoming an integral part of the company's senior-leadership team. I would be surprised if, after receiving Denton's proposal, she didn't decide to stay at Delarks.

When Garcia is back on board, Denton should turn to the rest of the senior managers. Holding an off-site session dedicated to sharing the senior group's knowledge about Delarks and defining the innovations needed to take the company to the next level would set things right quickly. I would strongly recommend that Denton hire a facilitator to help him run the session. He doesn't need a repeat of the town meeting. But the senior management team probably will be no larger than 15 people, and he can use the meeting to bring them together. The way he announces the stock option plan, for example, can help bond the group.

The key will be letting his managers know that he understands how Delarks fits in with their careers and with their lives in general, and that their experience should be both challenging and enjoyable. And he should impress upon them that he wants them to become the agents of a new culture that travels down through the organization.

Third, Create a Permanent Communication Process for all Delarks Employees

When I was CEO of Diner's Club, we had a successful program, and my suggestions stem from that. Denton should start a program called Take Stock in Delarks. If he follows my first recommendation, all Delarks employees will be stockholders and thus will be doubly interested in the company. To capitalize on that interest, he should issue a quarterly report on progress and challenges and then use the reports as a vehicle to generate discussions in individual stores. Subsequently, he can report on what he has learned and any employee ideas he has implemented, thus strengthening the connection between management and staff. Denton might also consider hosting an annual meeting or celebration as part of the program.

It will probably be a couple of years before the program takes hold—that is, before employees believe that the program isn't a gimmick. But if Denton takes my first two suggestions to heart, resolves to keep his focus on the future, and stops playing the lone ranger, morale should improve to the point that it mirrors those amazing turnaround numbers.

RICHARD MANNING *is the former editor of the* Boston Business Journal *and* New England Business *magazine. He is now a writer, editor, and consultant north of Boston.*

Denton needs to start all over again where he should have started in the first place: with his employees. And he needs to start with a display of honesty and forthrightness that so far has been incredibly lacking on his part.

The first thing he has to do is stop the bleeding. He has to send out a companywide memo that says two things: the layoffs are over, period, and I'll soon be visiting all 28 stores to meet with all the company's employees. If a copy of the memo ends up on page one of the next day's *Chicago Tribune*, well, that's simply a risk that Denton will have to take. His main problem has been isolation, after all,

Denton has to send out a memo that says the layoffs are over, period.

and anything that will bring him closer to his workforce will redound to the company's benefit. Even a press leak.

Denton needs to explain to his people in the memo that from the outset he had the equation upside down. The memo might look something like this:

"I felt that the way to turn the company around lay along the course of improving infrastructure, improving the product, and improving merchandising. And I was wrong in that assumption, because the assumption ignored the development of the company's most important assets: its employees.

"I realized this suddenly over the last few days when I learned that the head of merchandising was leaving, the head of HR was totally demoralized, and the chief of sales-associate training was poised to jump. I'd become so enmeshed in the balance sheet that I thought I could take the pulse of the company's most important assets by commissioning something as preposterous as an employee attitude survey. Such surveys are nothing but an invitation to dissemble, shrug, and flatter, and they often have no bearing on reality.

The memo might say this: "If the company's assets decide to vote with their feet, there will be no company left."

"What I have ignored all along is that in any corporation, large or small, the most important assets all wear shoes. They walk if you tell them to—as I've told 3,000 to do in the past year—or they walk if they're scared for their jobs. No steel mill, no law firm, no clothing retailer will be able to prosper if the assets that wear shoes are not managed the same way a prudent manager manages merchandising, infrastructure, and other parts of the business.

"This has been my greatest failing so far. In admitting that, I am putting my rear where I know everyone else's been all along: on the line. I should have been in Peoria and Bismarck and Madison talking with employees at the very outset, but I was not. I've been relying on outside consultants and managing in the splendid isolation of the eighteenth floor. And I've just come to the terrible realization that no matter what I do with the ledgers, if the company's assets decide to vote with their feet, there will be no company left. Dresses don't sell dresses. People sell dresses. People unload trucks. People stock stockrooms. People work cash registers.

"I've been blissfully ignorant of those truths for the past year, and it's my fault that morale is low and that people are talking about leaving in droves. To get things back to where they should be, Thomas Wazinsky, our head of HR, will organize employee feedback circles at each of the stores. The purpose of the circles will be to come up with ideas about how to make the company work better and to let employees know they have a real say in how the company operates. Store managers will present the circles' findings at monthly meetings at headquarters in Chicago.

"'Meaningful work,' to quote William Butler Yeats, 'is not the filling of a pail but the lighting of a fire.' I want Delarks people to know they can light fires at the company."

GUN DENHART *is founder and chair of Hanna Andersson Corporation, a children's clothing direct-mail company in Portland, Oregon.*

I don't believe that all is lost for Denton. At least not yet. But if he is to save Delarks, he must act fast, and his first priority must be rebuilding his employees' trust—in him and in the company.

First, I would suggest that he try again to meet with small groups of employees throughout the organization. He must be honest with them. No manager can promise a completely rosy future, and so he can't guarantee that there will never be another layoff at Delarks. But he should tell them that if the need ever arises again—if Delarks finds itself in a position in which downsizing is the only way to ensure survival—the situation will be handled much, much differently. And he should promise that employees will be kept up-to-date on the company's performance so that they will never again be blindsided.

It might be a good idea if Denton began these meetings with an apology. And at some point in the meeting, perhaps after he has assured people that there will be no more layoffs in the current restructuring, he should give them a chance to talk. People need to show their emotions, and Denton should let them do so without getting defensive. He should just listen until everyone who wants to speak has had a say.

I realize that that will be very difficult for him. He does not strike me as the kind of person who is sensitive in that way—who knows when to talk and when to listen. But perhaps he can prepare a bit beforehand—by role-playing with someone, for example—or at least make sure that his HR director is by his side at the meetings to raise a warning finger if he begins to get defensive or to talk over his employees.

Denton must understand, before hosting these meetings, that people are going to be very angry and that given the opportunity, in a safe forum, they will vent their true feelings. But he must also understand that anger is not going to be the only emotion fueling the storm. The employees who remain at Delarks are probably feeling quite a bit of guilt as well. After all, some of their closest friends—people with lifelong careers at the company—are now looking for work, while they still collect their pay.

Delarks employees should know if the stores are doing well or poorly—and why.

He must be ready to acknowledge that guilt and to take on some of it as his own.

When a meeting is over, Denton should hand out a letter to each employee that confirms his apology and his assurance that such a mismanaged downsizing will never again occur. That Denton means what he says and is ready to stand by his word must be made very real to everyone who attends.

The meetings are just a start. To follow through on his promises, Denton must change his management style. Specifically, that means visiting his stores on a regular basis. Getting to know employees' names and histories. Keeping people informed about the state of the business. Delarks employees should know if the stores are doing well or poorly. They should know why, and they should have a way to tell Denton what works at Delarks and what does not. In other words, they must be active participants in Denton's strategy for success, not just tools.

Denton's new management style must also include a commitment to communication—in both directions—with his senior management team. It is unconscionable that he did not inform his HR director or the manager in Madison that he was going to shut down that store. Denton has a great problem with trust. He has to realize that none of his employees will ever trust him unless he begins to trust them.

At least Denton realizes that something is dreadfully wrong at Delarks, and he wants to make things right. To that end, I would recommend that he contact Business for Social Responsibility, an organization based in San Francisco whose mission is to help managers achieve commercial success while maintaining the highest possible respect for people, the community, and the environment. With that help, and with some hard work, he may be able to salvage what was once a strong, positive company culture.

SAUL GELLERMAN *is a management psychologist in Irving, Texas, and the former dean of the Graduate School of Management at the University of Dallas.*

I'd fault Delarks's board of directors more than Denton for what looks like an impending disaster. Denton is a former store manager with no prior experience as a CEO. Without an informed mentor—someone who can ask tough questions and demand thoughtful answers—an inexperienced CEO can turn into a loose cannon, as Denton did.

There's no evidence of oversight by the board on Denton's decisions. It was content to look at the numbers, never inquiring whether they were sustainable or what the costs and risks of achieving them were. In brief, the board's governance was superficial and helped create this looming fiasco.

That said, the immediate question is, What's best for Delarks now?

In the short run, nothing is going to change the fact that Delarks lacks an effective leader. Denton lost much of his credibility when he axed the entire Madison store without warning. That shock made the isolated gripes of the disaffected few suddenly seem all too valid to the previously silent majority. It left the survivors anxious and cynical. After the Madison massacre, they probably lived in dread of Fridays. And after the St. Paul meeting, where Denton did more preaching than listening, they most likely lost all faith in the CEO.

The company still needs Denton's strategic guidance, but it needs someone else to implement his strategy on a day-to-day basis. In brief, Delarks needs someone to front for Denton, someone the frontline troops will believe.

The only senior executive in the case who could play that role convincingly is the head of HR, Wazinsky. His job title should be changed to executive vice president. But Denton should make this appointment with his eyes open, because Wazinsky—although he may have the respect of Delarks's employees—was not a strong HR director.

First, he settled for an amateurish employee-attitude survey. His consultants focused on a side issue—how morale at Delarks compared with that of other downsizing firms—and never got down to the key question: What issues were driving the "disaffection" that burst out of its "pockets" like a virus when Denton made his big blunder and closed the Madison store?

Second, there is no evidence that Wazinsky warned Denton that Delarks would be wide open to an age discrimination suit if he based mass layoffs on anything but performance. Firing "several hundred longtime saleswomen" like Mae Collier could come back to haunt Denton in ways that he fails to recognize.

Nevertheless, the appointment of Wazinsky would at least temporarily calm a very troubled organization. The message Wazinsky should try to convey is that while the good old days are gone forever, the company will cling to its original core values—decency and respect for each employee—even as it sheds some outdated values—the guaranteed job security and disregard for change that characterized the old Delarks.

Keeping Denton behind the scenes is a first step, but not the last. To rescue Denton's career at Delarks, the board's chair would have to intervene. Specifically, he or she would have to insist that Denton agree to cooperate with a consultant of the chair's choosing. In other words, Denton would have to want to fight on at Delarks so much that he would be willing to work with an outsider to learn a new management style.

If Denton does not agree to this course of action, the board would be better off owning up to its mistake. It should buy out his contract and shop around for a more thoughtful CEO. Of course, that implies major disruptions on the board itself. But that's the price of looking only at results and ignoring how they were achieved.

Fortunately, Denton already seems open to change. He's upset and knows that he's in trouble, both of which are good signs. They mean he's beginning to face the possibility that his own decisions are at the root of his difficulties.

One final point. Whenever you contemplate firing people, whether you're letting a single individual go or carrying out a massive downsizing, the most important consideration is always this: How will your decision affect the survivors? If morale plummets, you could lose your best people and get only the minimum effort from those left behind. In short, no economic gains for a lot of psychological pain.

Originally published in September–October 1998
Reprint 98510

How Resilience Works

DIANE L. COUTU

Executive Summary

WHY DO SOME PEOPLE BOUNCE back from life's
hardships while others despair? HBR senior editor Diane
Coutu looks at the nature of individual and organizational resilience, issues that have gained special urgency
in light of the recent terrorist attacks, war, and recession.
In the business arena, resilience has found its way onto
the list of qualities sought in employees. As one of
Coutu's interviewees puts it, "More than education, more
than experience, more than training, a person's level of
resilience will determine who succeeds and who fails."

Theories abound about what produces resilience, but
three fundamental characteristics seem to set resilient
people and companies apart from others. One or two of
these qualities make it possible to bounce back from
hardship, but true resilience requires all three.

The first characteristic is the capacity to accept and face down reality. In looking hard at reality, we prepare ourselves to act in ways that allow us to endure and survive hardships: We train ourselves how to survive before we ever have to do so.

Second, resilient people and organizations possess an ability to find meaning in some aspects of life. And values are just as important as meaning; value systems at resilient companies change very little over the long haul and are used as scaffolding in times of trouble.

The third building block of resilience is the ability to improvise. Within an arena of personal capabilities or company rules, the ability to solve problems without the usual or obvious tools is a great strength.

W HEN I BEGAN MY CAREER in journalism—I was a reporter at a national magazine in those days—there was a man I'll call Claus Schmidt. He was in his mid-fifties, and to my impressionable eyes, he was the quintessential newsman: cynical at times, but unrelentingly curious and full of life, and often hilariously funny in a sandpaper-dry kind of way. He churned out hard-hitting cover stories and features with a speed and elegance I could only dream of. It always astounded me that he was never promoted to managing editor.

But people who knew Claus better than I did thought of him not just as a great newsman but as a quintessential survivor, someone who had endured in an environment often hostile to talent. He had lived through at least three major changes in the magazine's leadership, losing most of his best friends and colleagues on the way.

At home, two of his children succumbed to incurable illnesses, and a third was killed in a traffic accident. Despite all this—or maybe because of it—he milled around the newsroom day after day, mentoring the cub reporters, talking about the novels he was writing— always looking forward to what the future held for him.

Why do some people suffer real hardships and not falter? Claus Schmidt could have reacted very differently. We've all seen that happen: One person cannot seem to get the confidence back after a layoff; another, persistently depressed, takes a few years off from life after her divorce. The question we would all like answered is, Why? What exactly is that quality of resilience that carries people through life?

It's a question that has fascinated me ever since I first learned of the Holocaust survivors in elementary school. In college, and later in my studies as an affiliate scholar at the Boston Psychoanalytic Society and Institute, I returned to the subject. For the past several months, however, I have looked on it with a new urgency, for it seems to me that the terrorism, war, and recession of recent months have made understanding resilience more important than ever. I have considered both the nature of individual resilience and what makes some organizations as a whole more resilient than others. Why do some people and some companies buckle under pressure? And what makes others bend and ultimately bounce back?

My exploration has taught me much about resilience, although it's a subject none of us will ever understand fully. Indeed, resilience is one of the great puzzles of human nature, like creativity or the religious instinct. But in sifting through psychological research and in reflecting on the many stories of resilience I've heard, I have seen a little more deeply into the hearts and minds of people like Claus Schmidt and, in doing so, looked more deeply into the human psyche as well.

The Buzz About Resilience

Resilience is a hot topic in business these days. Not long ago, I was talking to a senior partner at a respected consulting firm about how to land the very best MBAs—the name of the game in that particular industry. The partner, Daniel Savageau (not his real name), ticked off a long list of qualities his firm sought in its hires: intelligence, ambition, integrity, analytic ability, and so on. "What about resilience?" I asked. "Well, that's very popular right now," he said. "It's the new buzzword. Candidates even tell us they're resilient; they volunteer the information. But frankly, they're just too young to know that about themselves. Resilience is something you realize you have *after* the fact."

"More than education, more than experience, more than training, a person's level of resilience will determine who succeeds and who fails. That's true in the cancer ward, it's true in the Olympics, and it's true in the boardroom."

"But if you could, would you test for it?" I asked. "Does it matter in business?"

Savageau paused. He's a man in his late forties and a success personally and professionally. Yet it hadn't been a smooth ride to the top. He'd started his life as a poor French Canadian in Woonsocket, Rhode Island, and had lost his father at six. He lucked into a football scholarship but was kicked out of Boston University twice for drinking. He turned his life around in his twenties, mar-

ried, divorced, remarried, and raised five children. Along
the way, he made and lost two fortunes before helping to
found the consulting firm he now runs. "Yes, it does matter," he said at last. "In fact, it probably matters more
than any of the usual things we look for." In the course of
reporting this article, I heard the same assertion time
and again. As Dean Becker, the president and CEO of
Adaptiv Learning Systems, a four-year-old company in
King of Prussia, Pennsylvania, that develops and delivers
programs about resilience training, puts it: "More than
education, more than experience, more than training, a
person's level of resilience will determine who succeeds
and who fails. That's true in the cancer ward, it's true in
the Olympics, and it's true in the boardroom."

Academic research into resilience started about 40
years ago with pioneering studies by Norman Garmezy,
now a professor emeritus at the University of Minnesota
in Minneapolis. After studying why many children of
schizophrenic parents did not suffer psychological illness
as a result of growing up with them, he concluded that a
certain quality of resilience played a greater role in men-
tal health than anyone had previously suspected.

Today, theories abound about what makes resilience.
Looking at Holocaust victims, Maurice Vanderpol, a
former president of the Boston Psychoanalytic Society
and Institute, found that many of the healthy survivors
of concentration camps had what he calls a "plastic
shield." The shield was comprised of several factors,
including a sense of humor. Often the humor was black,
but nonetheless it provided a critical sense of perspective. Other core characteristics that helped included the
ability to form attachments to others and the possession
of an inner psychological space that protected the survivors from the intrusions of abusive others. Research

about other groups uncovered different qualities associated with resilience. The Search Institute, a Minneapolis-based nonprofit organization that focuses on resilience and youth, found that the more resilient kids have an uncanny ability to get adults to help them out. Still other research showed that resilient inner-city youth often have talents such as athletic abilities that attract others to them.

Many of the early theories about resilience stressed the role of genetics. Some people are just born resilient, so the arguments went. There's some truth to that, of course, but an increasing body of empirical evidence shows that resilience—whether in children, survivors of concentration camps, or businesses back from the brink—can be learned. For example, George Vaillant, the director of the Study of Adult Development at Harvard Medical School in Boston, observes that within various groups studied during a 60-year period, some people became markedly more resilient over their lifetimes. Other psychologists claim that unresilient people more easily develop resiliency skills than those with head starts.

Most of the resilience theories I encountered in my research make good common sense. But I also observed that almost all the theories overlap in three ways. Resilient people, they posit, possess three characteristics: a staunch acceptance of reality; a deep belief, often buttressed by strongly held values, that life is meaningful; and an uncanny ability to improvise. You can bounce back from hardship with just one or two of these qualities, but you will only be truly resilient with all three. These three characteristics hold true for resilient organizations as well. Let's take a look at each of them in turn.

Facing Down Reality

A common belief about resilience is that it stems from
an optimistic nature. That's true but only as long as
such optimism doesn't distort your sense of reality. In
extremely adverse situations, rose-colored thinking can
actually spell disaster. This point was made poignantly
to me by management researcher and writer Jim Collins,
who happened upon this concept while researching *Good
to Great*, his book on how companies transform themselves out of mediocrity. Collins had a hunch (an exactly
wrong hunch) that resilient companies were filled with
optimistic people. He tried out that idea on Admiral Jim
Stockdale, who was held prisoner and tortured by the
Vietcong for eight years.

Collins recalls: "I asked Stockdale: 'Who didn't make it
out of the camps?' And he said, 'Oh, that's easy. It was
the optimists. They were the ones who said we were
going to be out by Christmas. And then they said we'd be
out by Easter and then out by Fourth of July and out by
Thanksgiving, and then it was Christmas again.' Then
Stockdale turned to me and said, 'You know, I think they
all died of broken hearts.'"

In the business world, Collins found the same unblink-
ing attitude shared by executives at all the most successful companies he studied. Like Stockdale, resilient people
have very sober and down-to-earth views of those parts
of reality that matter for survival. That's not to say that
optimism doesn't have its place: In turning around a
demoralized sales force, for instance, conjuring a sense
of possibility can be a very powerful tool. But for bigger
challenges, a cool, almost pessimistic, sense of reality is
far more important.

Perhaps you're asking yourself, "Do I truly understand—and accept—the reality of my situation? Does my
organization?" Those are good questions, particularly
because research suggests most people slip into denial as
a coping mechanism. Facing reality, really facing it, is
grueling work. Indeed, it can be unpleasant and often
emotionally wrenching. Consider the following story of
organizational resilience, and see what it means to confront reality.

Prior to September 11, 2001, Morgan Stanley, the
famous investment bank, was the largest tenant in the
World Trade Center. The company had some 2,700
employees working in the south tower on 22 floors
between the 43rd and the 74th. On that horrible day, the
first plane hit the north tower at 8:46 am, and Morgan
Stanley started evacuating just one minute later, at 8:47
am. When the second plane crashed into the south tower
15 minutes after that, Morgan Stanley's offices were
largely empty. All told, the company lost only seven
employees despite receiving an almost direct hit.

Of course, the organization was just plain lucky to be
in the second tower. Cantor Fitzgerald, whose offices
were hit in the first attack, couldn't have done anything
to save its employees. Still, it was Morgan Stanley's hard-
nosed realism that enabled the company to benefit from
its luck. Soon after the 1993 attack on the World Trade
Center, senior management recognized that working in
such a symbolic center of U.S. commercial power made
the company vulnerable to attention from terrorists and
possible attack.

With this grim realization, Morgan Stanley launched
a program of preparedness at the micro level. Few companies take their fire drills seriously. Not so Morgan
Stanley, whose VP of security for the Individual Investor

Group, Rick Rescorla, brought a military discipline to the job. Rescorla, himself a highly resilient, decorated Vietnam vet, made sure that people were fully drilled about what to do in a catastrophe. When disaster struck on September 11, Rescorla was on a bullhorn telling Morgan Stanley employees to stay calm and follow their well-practiced drill, even though some building supervisors were telling occupants that all was well. Sadly, Rescorla himself, whose life story has been widely covered in recent months, was one of the seven who didn't make it out.

"When you're in financial services where so much depends on technology, contingency planning is a major part of your business," says President and COO Robert G. Scott. But Morgan Stanley was prepared for the very toughest reality. It had not just one, but three, recovery sites where employees could congregate and business could take place if work locales were ever disrupted. "Multiple backup sites seemed like an incredible extravagance on September 10," concedes Scott. "But on September 12, they seemed like genius."

Maybe it was genius; it was undoubtedly resilience at work. The fact is, when we truly stare down reality, we prepare ourselves to act in ways that allow us to endure and survive extraordinary hardship. We train ourselves how to survive before the fact.

The Search for Meaning

The ability to see reality is closely linked to the second building block of resilience, the propensity to make meaning of terrible times. We all know people who, under duress, throw up their hands and cry, "How can this be happening to me?" Such people see themselves as victims, and living through hardship carries no lessons for them. But resilient people devise constructs about their suffering to create some sort of meaning for themselves and others.

I have a friend I'll call Jackie Oiseaux who suffered repeated psychoses over a ten-year period due to an undiagnosed bipolar disorder. Today, she holds down a big job in one of the top publishing companies in the country, has a family, and is a prominent member of her church community. When people ask her how she bounced back from her crises, she runs her hands through her hair. "People sometimes say, 'Why me?' But I've always said, 'Why *not* me?' True, I lost many things during my illness," she says, "but I found many more—incredible friends who saw me through the bleakest times and who will give meaning to my life forever."

This dynamic of meaning making is, most researchers agree, the way resilient people build bridges from present-day hardships to a fuller, better constructed future. Those bridges make the present manageable, for lack of a better word, removing the sense that the present is overwhelming. This concept was beautifully articulated by Viktor E. Frankl, an Austrian psychiatrist and an Auschwitz survivor. In the midst of staggering suffering, Frankl invented "meaning therapy," a humanistic therapy technique that helps individuals make the kinds of decisions that will create significance in their lives.

In his book *Man's Search for Meaning*, Frankl described the pivotal moment in the camp when he developed meaning therapy. He was on his way to work one day, worrying whether he should trade his last cigarette for a bowl of soup. He wondered how he was going to work with a new foreman whom he knew to be particularly sadistic. Suddenly, he was disgusted by just how trivial and meaningless his life had become. He real-

ized that to survive, he had to find some purpose. Frankl
did so by imagining himself giving a lecture after the war
on the psychology of the concentration camp, to help
outsiders understand what he had been through.
Although he wasn't even sure he would survive, Frankl
created some concrete goals for himself. In doing so, he
succeeded in rising above the sufferings of the moment.
As he put it in his book: "We must never forget that we
may also find meaning in life even when confronted with
a hopeless situation, when facing a fate that cannot be
changed."

Frankl's theory underlies most resilience coaching in
business. Indeed, I was struck by how often businesspeople referred to his work. "Resilience training—what we
call hardiness—is a way for us to help people construct
meaning in their everyday lives," explains Salvatore R.
Maddi, a University of California, Irvine psychology professor and the director of the Hardiness Institute in New-
port Beach, California. "When people realize the power
of resilience training, they often say, 'Doc, is this what
psychotherapy is?' But psychotherapy is for people
whose lives have fallen apart badly and need repair. We
see our work as showing people life skills and attitudes.
Maybe those things should be taught at home, maybe
they should be taught in schools, but they're not. So we
end up doing it in business."

Yet the challenge confronting resilience trainers is
often more difficult than we might imagine. Meaning can
be elusive, and just because you found it once doesn't
mean you'll keep it or find it again. Consider Aleksandr
Solzhenitsyn, who survived the war against the Nazis,
imprisonment in the gulag, and cancer. Yet when he
moved to a farm in peaceful, safe Vermont, he could not
cope with the "infantile West." He was unable to discern
any real meaning in what he felt to be the destructive

and irresponsible freedom of the West. Upset by his critics, he withdrew into his farmhouse, behind a locked fence, seldom to be seen in public. In 1994, a bitter man, Solzhenitsyn moved back to Russia.

Since finding meaning in one's environment is such an important aspect of resilience, it should come as no surprise that the most successful organizations and people possess strong value systems. Strong values infuse an environment with meaning because they offer ways to interpret and shape events. While it's popular these days to ridicule values, it's surely no coincidence that the most resilient organization in the world has been the Catholic Church, which has survived wars, corruption, and schism for more than 2,000 years, thanks largely to its immutable set of values. Businesses that survive also have their creeds, which give them purposes beyond just making money. Strikingly, many companies describe their value systems in religious terms. Pharmaceutical giant Johnson & Johnson, for instance, calls its value system, set out in a document given to every new employee at orientation, the Credo. Parcel company UPS talks constantly about its Noble Purpose.

Value systems at resilient companies change very little over the years and are used as scaffolding in times of trouble. UPS Chairman and CEO Mike Eskew believes that the Noble Purpose helped the company to rally after the agonizing strike in 1997. Says Eskew: "It was a hugely difficult time, like a family feud. Everyone had close friends on both sides of the fence, and it was tough for us to pick sides. But what

Resilience is neither ethically good nor bad. It is merely the skill and the capacity to be robust under conditions of enormous stress and change.

saved us was our Noble Purpose. Whatever side people were on, they all shared a common set of values. Those values are core to us and never change; they frame most of our important decisions. Our strategy and our mission may change, but our values never do."

The religious connotations of words like "credo," "values," and "noble purpose," however, should not be confused with the actual content of the values. Companies can hold ethically questionable values and still be very resilient. Consider Phillip Morris, which has demonstrated impressive resilience in the face of increasing unpopularity. As Jim Collins points out, Phillip Morris has very strong values, although we might not agree with them—for instance, the value of "adult choice." But there's no doubt that Phillip Morris executives believe strongly in its values, and the strength of their beliefs sets the company apart from most of the other tobacco companies. In this context, it is worth noting that resilience is neither ethically good nor bad. It is merely the skill and the capacity to be robust under conditions of enormous stress and change. As Viktor Frankl wrote: "On the average, only those prisoners could keep alive who, after years of trekking from camp to camp, had lost all scruples in their fight for existence; they were prepared to use every means, honest and otherwise, even brutal. . . , in order to save themselves. We who have come back . . . we know: The best of us did not return."

Values, positive or negative, are actually more important for organizational resilience than having resilient people on the payroll. If resilient employees are all interpreting reality in different ways, their decisions and actions may well conflict, calling into doubt the survival of their organization. And as the weakness of an organization becomes apparent, highly resilient individuals are more likely to jettison the organization than to imperil their own survival.

Ritualized Ingenuity

The third building block of resilience is the ability to make do with whatever is at hand. Psychologists follow the lead of French anthropologist Claude Levi-Strauss in calling this skill bricolage.[1] Intriguingly, the roots of that word are closely tied to the concept of resilience, which literally means "bouncing back." Says Levi-Strauss: "In its old sense, the verb *bricoler* . . . was always used with reference to some extraneous movement: a ball rebounding, a dog straying, or a horse swerving from its direct course to avoid an obstacle."

Bricolage in the modern sense can be defined as a kind of inventiveness, an ability to improvise a solution to a problem without proper or obvious tools or materials. *Bricoleurs* are always tinkering—building radios from household effects or fixing their own cars. They make the most of what they have, putting objects to unfamiliar uses. In the concentration camps, for example, resilient inmates knew to pocket pieces of string or wire whenever they found them. The string or wire might later become useful—to fix a pair of shoes, perhaps, which in freezing conditions might make the difference between life and death.

When situations unravel, bricoleurs muddle through, imagining possibilities where others are confounded. I have two friends, whom I'll call Paul Shields and Mike Andrews, who were roommates throughout their college years. To no one's surprise, when they graduated, they set up a business together, selling educational materials to schools, businesses, and consulting firms. At first, the company was a great success, making both founders paper millionaires. But the recession of the early 1990s hit the company hard, and many core clients fell away. At the same time, Paul experienced a bitter divorce and a depression that made it impossible for him to work. Mike offered to buy Paul out but was instead slapped with a lawsuit claiming that Mike was trying to steal the business. At this point, a less resilient person might have just walked away from the mess. Not Mike. As the case wound through the courts, he kept the company going any way he could—constantly morphing the business until he found a model that worked: going into joint ventures to sell English-language training materials to Russian and Chinese companies. Later, he branched off into publishing newsletters for clients. At one point, he was even writing video scripts for his competitors. Thanks to all this bricolage, by the time the lawsuit was settled in his favor, Mike had an entirely different, and much more solid, business than the one he had started with.

Bricolage can be practiced on a higher level as well. Richard Feynman, winner of the 1965 Nobel Prize in physics, exemplified what I like to think of as intellectual bricolage. Out of pure curiosity, Feynman made himself an expert on cracking safes, not only looking at the mechanics of safecracking but also cobbling together psychological insights about people who used safes and set the locks. He cracked many of the safes at Los Alamos, for instance, because he guessed that theoretical physicists would not set the locks with random code numbers they might forget but would instead use a sequence with mathematical significance. It turned out that the three safes containing all the secrets to the atomic bomb were set to the same mathematical constant, e, whose first six digits are 2.71828.

Resilient organizations are stuffed with bricoleurs, though not all of them, of course, are Richard Feynmans. Indeed, companies that survive regard improvisation as a core skill. Consider UPS, which empowers its drivers to do whatever it takes to deliver packages on time. Says CEO Eskew: "We tell our employees to get the job done. If that means they need to improvise, they improvise. Otherwise we just couldn't do what we do every day. Just think what can go wrong: a busted traffic light, a flat tire, a bridge washed out. If a snowstorm hits Louisville tonight, a group of people will sit together and discuss how to handle the problem. Nobody tells them to do that. They come together because it's our tradition to do so."

That tradition meant that the company was delivering parcels in southeast Florida just one day after Hurricane Andrew devastated the region in 1992, causing billions of dollars in damage. Many people were living in their cars because their homes had been destroyed, yet UPS drivers and managers sorted packages at a diversion site and made deliveries even to those who were stranded in their cars. It was largely UPS's improvisational skills that enabled it to keep functioning after the catastrophic hit. And the fact that the company continued on gave others a sense of purpose or meaning amid the chaos.

Improvisation of the sort practiced by UPS, however, is a far cry from unbridled creativity. Indeed, much like the military, UPS lives on rules and regulations. As Eskew says: "Drivers always put their keys in the same place. They close the doors the same way. They wear their uniforms the same way. We are a company of precision." He believes that although they may seem stifling, UPS's rules were what allowed the company to bounce back immediately after Hurricane Andrew, for they enabled people to focus on the one or two fixes they needed to make in order to keep going.

Eskew's opinion is echoed by Karl E. Weick, a professor of organizational behavior at the University of Michigan Business School in Ann Arbor and one of the most respected thinkers on organizational psychology. "There is good evidence that when people are put under pressure, they regress to their most habituated ways of responding," Weick has written. "What we do not expect under life-threatening pressure is creativity." In other words, the rules and regulations that make some companies appear less creative may actually make them more resilient in times of real turbulence.

CLAUS SCHMIDT, THE NEWSMAN I mentioned earlier, died about five years ago, but I'm not sure I could have interviewed him about his own resilience even if he were alive. It would have felt strange, I think, to ask him, "Claus, did you really face down reality? Did you make meaning out of your hardships? Did you improvise your recovery after each professional and personal disaster?" He may not have been able to answer. In my experience, resilient people don't often describe themselves that way. They shrug off their survival stories and very often assign them to luck.

Obviously, luck does have a lot to do with surviving. It was luck that Morgan Stanley was situated in the south tower and could put its preparedness training to work. But being lucky is not the same as being resilient. Resilience is a reflex, a way of facing and understanding the world, that is deeply etched into a person's mind and soul. Resilient people and companies face reality with staunchness, make meaning of hardship instead of crying out in despair, and improvise solutions from thin air. Others do not. This is the nature of resilience, and we will never completely understand it.

Notes

1. See, e.g., Karl E. Weick, "The Collapse of Sensemaking in Organizations: The Mann Gulch Disaster," *Administrative Science Quarterly*, December 1993.

Originally published in May 2002
Reprint R0205B

The Trouble I've Seen

DAVID N. JAMES

Executive Summary

DAVID JAMES IS A PROFESSIONAL crisis manager. For almost 30 years, his job has been to rescue companies on the brink of bankruptcy. By the time he's called in, it's usually too late to save much for the shareholders. In almost every case, however, there is still a lot to salvage: Nearly all the companies James has managed continue to operate in some form. More than £2 billion have been repaid to banks and unsecured trade creditors. And more than 30,000 jobs have been saved.

The key to preserving value, James has found, is to resist the urge to try to regenerate cash from operating the business. In most cases, these companies have taken on far too much debt to ever sell their way out. Indeed, trying to expand operations beyond what the market would bear was what got them into trouble in the first place. James argues against waiting until the company is dead to break it up. A more effective course is to sell off valuable assets while the company is still a going concern.

In vivid and sometimes hair-raising detail, James recounts how he has discovered valuable assets in unexpected places, salvaging everything from airlines to soft-drink makers to Britain's Millennium Dome. He has a routine for accomplishing this, which involves locking up the checkbook on day one and, more often than not, firing the senior management. His is a cautionary tale for top executives who, it is clear, should be concentrating their efforts on never needing to call on him in the first place.

MY JOB IS TO RESCUE failing companies. As a professional crisis manager, I have been asked to take control, usually as executive chairman, of more than 90 companies, from retailers to airlines. Some numbered among Britain's larger publicly traded groups; others were smaller, privately held operations. All of them faced the imminent threat of bankruptcy.

By the time I am called in, it is usually too late to save much for the shareholders. In almost every case, however, there is still a lot to salvage. Nearly all the companies I have managed continue to operate in some form even today; bank debts totaling more than £1 billion have been repaid, around another £1 billion has been returned to unsecured trade creditors, and more than 30,000 jobs have been saved. Clearly, successful crisis management makes a big difference to the parties directly involved, and it can greatly reduce the economic impact of a company's collapse on the broader business community.

The profession has changed significantly over the years. When I started, there were only a half dozen or so of us, and we all concentrated, as I still do, on the bigger company collapses. Today, there are perhaps 100 or more people in the UK calling themselves turnaround specialists, the majority of them managing smaller cases. Large company or small, though, the principles of rescue are the same, and as I near the end of a long career, it is a good time to reflect on the lessons I have learned, some of which you may find quite surprising.

For a start, companies do not necessarily go wrong because they are in chronically difficult industries. Nor is it that their managers are hasty and overconfident in making decisions or cannot obtain capital on reasonable terms. Most of the failures I have dealt with occurred at companies with a track record of success, whose managers had detailed business plans and where capital was readily available at low rates.

I have found, though, that once a company hits trouble, many executives misdirect their efforts. Typically, they put all their energy into managing the company's cash flow when they should be addressing corporate structure and strategy. That may be because they find it hard to rethink the structures and strategies they themselves put in place. Whatever the reason, the consequences are usually the same. The rescue starts too late and accomplishes less than it should.

I do not mean, of course, that careful cash flow management is irrelevant to a corporate rescue, but I do believe that the rescuer's priorities must be elsewhere. In my experience, the key to a rescue usually lies in the company's balance sheet, and this is where I concentrate my efforts. Indeed, the deeper the trouble a company finds itself in, the more important it is to focus on the balance sheet, because a cash flow–driven rescue is unlikely to work fast enough to save the company. Nearly every once-successful company in the examples that follow had treasure buried somewhere in its books, and the realization of that value meant much more for its successful rescue than any relatively slow improvements in sales or costs could ever have done.

Let us begin by looking at what gets companies into trouble in the first place.

From Success to Disaster

The healthiest-looking companies are often the most likely to get into trouble. The dynamic usually unfolds this way. Delighted with the company's results, shareholders press management to grow by increasing production capacity, moving into new markets, or even making acquisitions, often backing up their demands with offers to fund more equity. At the same time, the company's banks are eager to lend to what they perceive to be a sure credit risk.

Competitors, however, are usually eyeing the very same opportunities. As they close in, they offer customers the chance to play the various companies off against one another. That places the incumbent's market share and margins under considerable pressure, leaving the company very exposed to a downturn. When it comes, as it inevitably does, the new factory or acquired subsidiary becomes a white elephant, as the company scrambles to cover its operating costs and higher production overhead. It struggles to service its by now much-increased debt, let alone maintain its dividend. Eventually, it ends up in breach of its borrowing covenants, which creates a major funding crisis. Once successful, the company now faces the imminent prospect of bankruptcy.

The risks are always greater if interest rates are low at the time the decision to expand is taken because the ready availability of credit makes it more likely that the company will fund the investment by borrowing. If interest rates then rise, the company will bear higher debt costs just when its margins are being squeezed. I have found, in fact, that companies have far greater problems repaying the capital incurred when they took advantage of low interest rates than they have dealing with the impact of higher rates on existing debt.

What triggers this dynamic? Investors must take some of the blame; shareholders who are used to seeing a company grow at a rate of 30% or so for several years in a row come to expect more of the same, placing enormous pressure on the management. The greatest responsibility, however, must rest with the managers themselves, who are far too prone to taking past success for granted and so are only too happy to go along with their investors. The more successful a company has been, the likelier it is to fall into the trap.

The danger is perhaps at its greatest after a change in management or after receipt of a cash windfall, which spurs conservative managers to take decisions they would never normally make. Mistakes can also arise when managers recognize that their business environment is changing but are not confident enough to trust their instincts and end up following advice they do not fully understand. When they pay a lot for the advice, they are even more inclined to take it. One or more of these factors have been responsible for nearly every corporate disaster I have been called in to manage.

The story of the Robinson Group, of which I became executive chairman in September 1998, perfectly illustrates how a change in management can trigger the dynamic of failure. A family-owned business that had been operating very profitably for about 40 years, Robinson was one of Britain's leading soft drink manufacturers, supplying private label drinks for retailers. It was the number two producer of dilute-to-taste fruit squashes, enjoying a solid 30% of the market. It also had a healthy share of the mineral water market, and supplied cola for brands such as Virgin. Based in Tenbury Wells, a country town, Robinson had relatively modest assets on paper; one of its principal production facilities was a converted railway station. It employed about 600 people.

Early in the 1990s, the second generation of the founding family took control. The new team believed that the recently completed formation of the single European market offered growth opportunities for a company with a solid home base. Further, Robinson seemed well positioned to make investments in growth since it was debt free. So the board decided to move the whole operation into a new, purpose-built factory near the center of the motorway network. The aim was to create an integrated production and distribution center on the site, financed by a £50 million bank loan. Robinson's top managers estimated that the move would increase the company's production capacity by more than 50%. At the same time, they expected distribution costs per unit to fall because of the new factory's improved accessibility. Finally, they thought the new factory could be run more or less nonstop, giving them a capacity utilization level of around 85%.

All this, though, assumed a healthy home market for Robinson's products. In fact, the domestic business was extremely vulnerable on several counts. First, only five customers—the main UK grocery chains—accounted for 80% of Robinson's sales. Second, demand for its largest and most profitable product line—dilute-to-taste squashes—was tailing off, as consumers switched to canned drinks and flavored waters. Robinson soon discovered that it could not even protect its margins, let alone improve them. Lack of demand for the extra volume also meant that Robinson did not have the economies of scale to drive the distribution savings.

To make matters worse, the competition was also creating new capacity. Both Princes, a subsidiary of Mitsubishi, and the large independent producer Macaws had already made major investments in production capacity, especially in the growing carbonated drink segment. In fact, capacity in that segment rose by almost 20% the year Robinson's factory came on-line. On top of all that, Robinson now had to carry the funding costs of the bank debt. The new management's decisions had led the company to the edge of bankruptcy in just three years.

Windfalls have much the same effect, as the case of LEP demonstrates. Between 1992 and 1995, I was chairman of the company, a British freight management organization with a worldwide staff of 15,000. LEP was a successful and long-established business, competing with a number of equally old and thriving businesses, mostly German and Swiss. It had a distinguished history; in the mid-nineteenth century, it transported gold bullion for the Bank of England, and it was the first freight company to use air transport. Like Robinson, LEP was virtually debt free.

The company's troubles began with a windfall capital gain of nearly £150 million from the development in 1985 of its property in the heart of the City of London, where its operations had been based since 1840. The company decided that the money offered a rare opportunity to increase its share of a traditionally very stable market, in which the production capacities and market shares of all the players were well entrenched.

Just like Robinson, LEP expanded by significantly upgrading its operations. One of the larger investments was made in its Austrian subsidiary, which had been generating steady annual profits of around £750,000 on a relatively small overhead. LEP now decided to build a £30 million freight conversion terminal for switching freight between the East European rail network and the West European road infrastructure. All told, LEP invested about £90 million in expanding its capacity in 32 different countries, including $45 million on a U.S. distribution network.

The decision could not have come at a worse time. Market capacity was about to explode. The line between freight management and express parcel delivery—hitherto separate businesses—was blurring, and the parcel companies saw freight management as a way to expand. To make matters worse, the new players—notably UPS and FedEx—had a much better grasp of the IT needs of the business than did LEP and its traditional competition. In this very different environment, LEP's projections for increased traffic were not realized, and the expanded overseas units moved heavily into the red. The Austrian subsidiary, for instance, started producing annual losses of around £3 million. The worst casualties were in the United States, where LEP's distribution acquisition lost $50 million in its first year. LEP had gone from windfall to free fall.

The LEP story also illustrates the dangers of relying on other people's expertise. In addition to expanding the core business, the new managers had decided to diversify, probably to reduce the company's dependence on freight, which was highly cyclical. They recognized, however, that they had little relevant experience, and so they recruited a team of executives with broader commercial expertise to manage an acquisition program. The new team, eager to demonstrate its worth, rapidly acquired the most extraordinary range of businesses. It bought engineering companies in South Africa, garment manufacturers in Hungary and Malta, extensive property interests in California, and even a one-third share in a Tanzanian gold mine. Inevitably, much of this ill-assorted and hastily assembled portfolio proved worthless.

The acquisition program, combined with the expansion of the core business, cost LEP a lot more than its £150 million windfall. Banks had been keen to open credit lines because they saw LEP as a cash-rich company with no debt and a long history of profitability, and LEP seized the opportunity. As a result, its debt rose to around £685 million from zero in just four years. In the end, the banks lost about half the value of their loans; the shareholders were wiped out.

Deferring to other people's expertise is most dangerous when a traditional company wants to compete in an emerging industry. I was recently called in on an unofficial basis to advise a company that had made a number of disastrous investments in new high-tech ventures. The company's senior board members had felt that they did not understand the "new economy" and had deferred almost completely to their younger colleagues, assuming that the younger generation knew what it was doing, which for a while seemed to be the case. Unfortunately, the board's reticence meant that the younger people were never really pushed to examine closely whether their judgment was commercially sound, and in due course the investments went sour.

Mining for Hidden Gold

What do you do when a company's bad decisions have come home to roost? Most turnaround practitioners focus on generating more cash through operations. They try to reestablish the company as an attractive going concern, in the hope of selling it more or less intact to another company. They are reluctant to take book losses on assets because they believe in an eventual trading recovery— that business will pick up and help assets recover value. Indeed, many struggling companies are not broken up until they have actually gone bankrupt. Unfortunately, the assets are then divorced from the markets or contracts they are intended to serve, and so they fetch less than they would if they had been sold out of an ongoing business. This is why I always work hard to convince lenders that their best return will come not from forcing bankruptcy but by helping the company stay solvent.

Businesses like Robinson and LEP are usually well beyond a trading recovery, and the only way to rescue any real value is to parcel them into separate packages of assets while they are still alive. These packages can then be sold to third parties, who may be willing to pay a premium if they do not have to take on the loss-making assets as well.

When I took over Robinson, it soon became clear that the company had no hope of even covering its operating costs through operating revenues, let alone repaying its debt. Not only did the market have too much capacity for the company to profit from its new facility, but the factory came on-line during an extended period of bad weather, which always hurts demand in the soft drink industry. Nonetheless, we convinced the banks to let us keep going long enough to repay the debts through asset sales before being forced into bankruptcy.

The Robinson Group had five trading subsidiaries. The main business was the unit making dilute-to-taste squashes and carbonated drinks in the new factory. Obviously, in the current climate, no one would pay much for a soft drink facility. What was worse, the purpose-built factory was ill-suited to alternative uses. We would have to sell it to somebody who was prepared to spend a lot of money converting the facility. Selling the factory would not realize enough cash to cover even half the debt. (That, too, is an important lesson. In creating a special-purpose asset like a factory, you must build in flexibility so you can get out of it if you need to.)

Where, then, was the treasure buried? The other units seemed to have little to offer. There was a reasonably solid plastic-bottle-blowing unit and another small business that made the forms from which the bottles were blown. Both could be sold at more or less their book value, but there was little scope for creating more value by converting the assets to some other purpose. All told, the realizable value of the factory and of Robinson's bottling businesses covered only about half of the loans outstanding.

That left two water businesses, whose prime assets were the water bore holes they were drawing upon. On the face of it, these businesses had little to offer, as their book value amounted to less than 6% of the bank debt. On looking a little more closely, however, we realized that one of the bores happened to tap into Europe's largest aquifer. Why was it worth only a couple of

By focusing on the assets, we saved the company; had we tried to trade out of the crisis, bankruptcy would have been inevitable.

million pounds, when far smaller ones from the same source had traded for ten times that amount? The reason, it seemed, was that the water's nitrate levels were—at 28 milligrams per liter—rather higher than the new EEC guidelines allowed for, and filtering would not be a cost-effective option.

We also noticed, however, that the company was only drawing water from this huge aquifer at a relatively shallow 55 meters. We decided to test the water at deeper levels, and for just £150,000 sunk a new test bore hole. The investment paid off; at 110 meters, we found that the nitrate content plunged to just five milligrams. On that basis, the water business was worth much more than its book value and attracted a lot of potential buyers, eventually realizing tens of millions of pounds. We settled the bank debts in full, allowing us to sell the factory at a large book loss, and the main remaining businesses could then all be sold as solvent, going concerns. By focusing on the assets, we saved the company from a bankruptcy that would have been inevitable had we tried to trade out of the crisis or tried to sell the entire business as an entity.

I had a similar experience in managing the Dan-Air rescue in 1991. Dan-Air was a once highly successful charter airline that had gotten into serious difficulties in the late 1980s. I was called in to take over as executive chairman and immediately undertook a detailed inspection of the company's assets. One of those was a jumbo-sized hangar, at London's Gatwick airport, which was on the books at £7 million. The hangar had limited operational value for Dan-Air, which principally flew smaller aircraft, but it was the only hangar at Gatwick capable of servicing a 747. It was certainly going to be valuable to other airlines. We eventually sold the hangar for £23 million. The next asset to go was the company's own engineering and maintenance arm, whose capacity far exceeded the needs of our 37 aircraft. We got £27 million for that business, while retaining an ongoing maintenance contract for our fleet.

In this case, we did not have to pay over the whole proceeds to the banks. Although we owed them £60 million, they were happy enough to accept just £21 million, representing the combined net book value of the assets. That left us with £29 million to put toward working capital, enabling us to survive the Gulf War despite losing an average of £750,000 for each of the war's 42 days. The banks had never expected to get any more than the book value from these assets, so that was the amount they had earmarked as cover for their loans. As long as no other assets were underwater relative to book, the surplus belonged to the company that had worked to realize it. I have often persuaded British banks to accept this argument and have had similar success in the United States.

The Routine for Rescue

Over the years, I have developed a fairly consistent routine for crisis management, which can be loosely summarized in seven rules. They govern the conditions under which I will accept an assignment and how I operate a company when I take over as executive chairman.

COMMISSION A SOLVENCY REPORT

First, as a condition of taking a company on, I insist that its board commission an investigative report by a major accounting firm, which obviously must not be the company's auditors. I always keep in close touch with the investigation, specifying its scope and then monitoring its progress. That allows me to form my own opinion as to whether, and how, the company can be salvaged. In the case of the Millennium Dome, a government-owned business I took charge of in September 2000, I actually managed the investigative exercise on behalf of the board, even though I had no status in the company at the time.

The report serves two purposes. First, it tells me how much extra cash the company needs to stay solvent. In the case of the Dome, the report demonstrated that the company would be insolvent within days without a capital injection of £47 million, which could come only from Britain's National Lottery. I did not take on the Dome until the National Lottery pledged the money. Second, the report also provides a comprehensive analysis of the company's balance sheet, its assets and long-term liabilities. So the day I walk in as chairman, I know exactly what I face.

GRAB THE CHECKBOOKS

What do I do on day one? I make sure no money goes out the door without my say-so. I have a vivid memory from Dan-Air, where I discovered that one purchasing manager had been so concerned about the controls we might put in place that he had bought three years' worth of plastic cups on the day we arrived just to make sure he had enough! That is the sort of panic spending you have got to watch out for. If you do nothing else on day one, lock up the checkbooks.

FIND THE HIDDEN HEROES

I then have to identify with whom I can work inside the company. Very often, these people do not come from existing top management but rather from the unit-head level. I have a fairly standard process for assessing the quality of these people.

First, I organize a meeting in which the unit heads sit around one big conference table. I ask them each to make a ten-minute pitch to describe their perception of their marketplace, their present problems, and their plans, which gives me an opportunity to see them in action. Typically at the end I say, "We want to present all of your businesses as going concerns in the most attractive way because that will be in everybody's best interest. Each of you has special problems. You people, for example, face deteriorating margins, falling volumes, and problems with your product range. Fine, but you have also got some solid assets, so write me your business plan as though you were presenting it to a purchaser. That will tell me what I need to know about your business and help me to sell it. It will also enable you to project yourselves as the continuing management. So we all share a common cause. I will admit to you that in preparing this report, you will also be helping me to know whether you are any good at your jobs, because when you have done your draft plan, you will review it with me, and I will subject it to very close scrutiny."

This tactic gives people a positive challenge. It invites them to demonstrate their strengths in businesses that they are supposed to know about. You find out what the problems in the businesses are because they cannot conceal them. It also sets the agenda for continuing close dialogue. I give them a very tight timetable: "I want to review the first draft within a week and go final in two weeks."

I am continually surprised by the number of hidden heroes I have found through this process and also just from walking around a company's facilities. Once, I took a talented foreman off the shop floor and turned him into the production director. Over the years, many of these people became members of my regular team for some time before moving on, either as independent crisis managers themselves or as CEOs in the conventional business world.

IF NECESSARY, SWEEP OUT THE OLD LEADERS

I always start with a strong desire to work with the existing top managers. They are usually experienced businesspeople with a deep knowledge of their industry. Unfortunately, in many cases, I have had to fire them because they seem to have a hard time accepting that they are no longer in control. They maintain their hope for some miracle solution and resist the rescuers in an effort to conceal their failure.

Typically, top managers try to insulate me from the line managers I need to work with. This dynamic was very much in evidence when I took over a major retail chain facing annual losses of about 17% of sales. The company comprised a number of independently managed brands, coordinated through a huge corporate center. The top executives at the center were highly experienced in retailing, an industry about which I knew very little, and I looked forward to their support.

On arrival, I convened a large meeting with the senior brand managers. The top executive team from the corporate center attended the meeting, which ended as usual with a request from me for business plans from the unit heads. Once that meeting was over, I made it clear that I would not seek to interfere in the day-to-day running of the business provided I was kept fully informed. I put myself discreetly around the corner, out of sight, where I could set up my separate unit to concentrate on the overall rescue strategy and financing plan.

I was hugely disappointed by the response. The meeting took place on a Tuesday, and by Friday I was beginning to believe that the corporate executives had told the unit heads to ignore my instructions completely. On Thursday the following week, I fired the chief corporate executives and put myself in as chairman of every one of the subsidiaries, despite my ignorance of retailing. I said to the units: "Tell me what you need, and I will help you." We sold every one of those businesses as a going concern, generating about £100 million, well in excess of the break-even values that many thought we would be lucky to get. We also saved 6,600 jobs.

Every time you walk through the door you say, "Please God, let this be a supportive management I can keep with me," but they rarely are. So usually you end up having to fire them.

Top management's denial often manifests itself in a very tangible way. When I took over at the Dome, for example, we found that the company had made little preparation for our arrival. They pointed us to a corner of the site offices that had no partitions, desks, or phones but did have a lot of dust and some mousetraps. However subconscious, this was an attempt to repel invaders. Fortunately, the Dome proved to be one of the rare cases where senior management did accept us, and our teams did gel remarkably well.

Every time you walk through the door you say, "Please God, let this be a supportive management I can keep with me," but they rarely are. So usually you end up having to fire them. About a fortnight is par for the course.

TAKE DECISIONS—EVEN WRONG ONES

One of the great executives of Ford, where I worked 35 years ago, used to say: "If you've got ten decisions to make and you spend all your time making just four, then you've made six wrong decisions." In fact, not taking a decision is worse than making the wrong one because it is often easier to manage your way out of a bad decision than to recover from the consequences of delay.

I made a number of wrong decisions during the Dan-Air rescue. One of them was to expand the company's initially small scheduled-route business in 1991, in the expectation that travel would pick up after the Gulf War. The alternative would have been to abandon it altogether and revert to just the charter business. Wrong decision though it was for the business at the time—the increase in demand did not pan out—we did end up owning a number of valuable travel routes. That made the company more attractive to outside buyers, in particular British Airways, which would never have purchased Dan-Air later had it still been predominantly a charter airline. Although my decision proved wrong, doing nothing would have been much worse.

ALWAYS HAVE A PLAN B

Behind every rescue stands a worried banker. He watches your every move; his approval is needed for any asset sale. Lose the sale, and his first instinct will be to trigger bankruptcy. You can never rely, therefore, on any one negotiation to sell an asset. You must have a contingency plan to do something else with the asset if the initial deal bombs. It must be clear to the bank that, even though Plan B may deliver less value, it will still yield more than a bankruptcy sale would.

My colleagues often say that by demanding contingency planning, I create an unnecessary workload and a sense of crisis when all is going well. It is no coincidence, however, that I have never yet lost a trading company to bankruptcy. A contingency plan is the guarantee of survival, and the day you cannot walk away from a negotiation is the day you will lose the company.

At Robinson, for instance, final closure with the company's trade creditors was wholly dependent upon a successful sale of the dilute-to-taste division. Unfortunately, there was only one possible buyer, which put the whole rescue at risk, even though the buyer involved showed no signs at any point of walking away. All the same, I forced my team to work for several nights and the weekend before the sale agreement date. I wanted them to come up with a backup plan to convince the banks that there would still be another route open that was better than bankruptcy. Fortunately, we did not have to try it.

GET MORE MONEY THAN YOU THINK YOU NEED

Rescues always need more money than you think, and you have to take every opportunity you can for getting extra cash. Perhaps my greatest career mistake came from not seizing such an opportunity in the Dan-Air rescue.

The company had managed to survive the Gulf War, and we had put together a business plan demonstrating that Dan-Air was a viable long-term trading proposition, provided airline traffic recovered quickly after the war. We estimated, though, that it needed about £56 million in new capital to help it through the first year. To test investor appetite, we put together a "pathfinder," a preplacement document for distribution to existing and potential new shareholders, positioning Dan-Air as a recovery play.

We went out with the document on a Thursday morning intending to do a five-day program of presentations to potential investors through Thursday, Friday, Monday, Tuesday, and Wednesday. By Friday night, I had received offers of £116 million at the suggested price. All weekend I agonized about the placement. I said to myself: "This is crazy: £56 million will work if everything goes perfectly, but nothing ever does. If I have already seen £116 million after talking to less than half the potential investors, it is likely we could get offered as much as £140 million. So why don't we up the price and go for £90 million instead? That will give me enough cash cover for an extra year, in case traffic does not pick up early enough, and still see me clear of the banks. This must be in everybody's interest." I went back to the board and our advisers on the Monday morning and told them what I thought.

They were adamantly opposed. After all the company had been through, they did not want to trade off the certainty of raising £56 million against the probability of raising more. Discussions went on all day, and in the end, because I was in a minority of one, I gave in. I will always regret that decision. If Dan-Air had sold just two more business-class tickets per flight in that first year—the equivalent of £30 million in revenue—it might well have survived as an independent operator, forcing British Airways or some other airline, a few years later, to pay a really high price for it. An extra £30 million on the placing would have done just as well.

I also learned from this experience that there comes a moment when a CEO has to trust his own gut instinct. In nine cases out of ten, the majority opinion will be right. Every so often, though—and most CEOs can sense when these moments of truth arrive—it is absolutely essential to exercise your prerogative and defy the collective wisdom of the board and its advisers. If I had stuck to my guns, I would have saved the shareholders the £56 million they had put up.

The Exhilaration of Rescue

As readers will probably have gathered by now, company doctoring is not for the fainthearted. It is, though, an exhilarating career, and I knew after my assignment nearly 30 years ago at ENM, an engineering company based in Tottenham in North London, that it was the lifetime career I was looking for. My brief was to supervise the sale of the business, which was scheduled to take place within a matter of weeks.

On my first day, the Tuesday after Christmas, my office windows were stoned, and my car was vandalized. On Wednesday, there was a pitched battle between the maintenance shop workers and the toolmakers. Later that day, I discovered that in August the company's largest customer had canceled his order, about one-fifth of annual output, but nobody had told the production staff, so we were horrendously overstocked. On Thursday, the payroll was robbed (an inside job), and the unions called a strike meeting. On Friday, the main boilers blew up, and it was almost a relief to have to send everybody home. Inevitably, the planned sale of ENM fell through, and I ended up running this company for two years. I had the time of my life. We eventually redesigned and relocated the factory, and reduced the workforce from 1,000 to 500, all with the union's support.

When the day comes for me to hang up my black bag, I shall look back on experiences like that with great satisfaction.

How Chapter 11 Destroys Industries

OVER THE YEARS, I have developed strong views on the efficacy of various countries' bankruptcy processes. The United States comes out quite poorly. Its famous Chapter 11 process, which protects a company from its past creditors and allows it to continue operating, ends up damaging entire industries.

By freeing a company from past obligations, Chapter 11 enables it to offer customers advantageous terms. This places it at a huge advantage relative to businesses that have continued to pay their creditors in full. They, as a result, lose customers to the Chapter 11 company, and the profitability of the whole industry declines, creating a real risk that the trouble will spread to other corporations. This is particularly dangerous for industries that are cash flow sensitive, where businesses can incur heavy creditor obligations.

The airline industry is a good example. Leasing an aircraft, let alone operating it, costs hundreds of thousands of dollars a month. When TWA and Continental ran into difficulties in the early 1990s, they were quickly put into Chapter 11 by their boards, which meant that they could continue to fly. Both of them operated on the transatlantic routes, the most profitable in the business. Since the only creditors they had to satisfy were new ones, they could undercut British Airways, Delta, American, and all the other airlines, which were not in such dire straits and which had no creditor protection. By invoking Chapter 11, therefore, TWA and Continental created an artificial price structure for the whole industry and undermined the good companies.

If Robinson had been able to seek Chapter 11-style creditor protection in the UK, it would almost certainly have survived, because it too could have undercut all its competitors. The resulting extra market share would have helped make the new factory profitable. In doing this, though, Robinson would have pushed Princes, Macaws, and its other competitors into Chapter 11 as well. The whole industry would have suffered, and a worse problem would have been created.

It is a mystery to me how the United States, which is normally so tough on competition issues, can at the same time sponsor laws that create such an advantage for failing businesses. The British government wants to introduce laws similar to Chapter 11 in the UK. I cannot think why.

Originally published in March 2002
Reprint R0203B

Cutting Costs Without Drawing Blood

TOM COPELAND

Executive Summary

WHEN LOOKING FOR WAYS TO CUT COSTS, most managers reach for the head-count hatchet, and the markets usually roar with approval. But a company can almost always create far more sustainable value by rigorously evaluating the small-ticket capital items that often get rubber-stamped. Drawing on his experience as a consultant and providing numerous anecdotes, the author contends that those "little" requests often prove to be gold plated or unnecessary.

A disciplined evaluation involves asking only eight questions and conducting postmortems—regular audits of units' capital spending. But the payoff is enormous. Because cutting the capital budget increases cash flow, the author argues that a permanent cut of just 15% in the planned level of capital spending could boost some companies' market capitalization by as much as 30%.

The first three questions—is this your investment to make? Does it really have to be new? How are our competitors meeting compliance needs?—are asked of operating managers as they assemble capital project requests. The next three are asked by senior managers of themselves and their colleagues as they examine proposals: Is the left hand duplicating investments made by the right? Are trade-offs between profits and capital spending well understood? Are there signs of budget massage? At the end of the review process, senior managers ask: Are we fully using shared assets? How fine-grained are our capacity measures? The author's suggestions for the post-mortem include searching for systematic problems with whole classes of expenditures and making sure audit teams come up with specific recommendations for change.

IN LOOKING FOR WAYS TO CUT COSTS—something most companies still need to do despite the good economic times—most managers reach for the head-count hatchet. There's good reason: the markets usually roar with approval. When Eastman Kodak, for example, announced three years ago that it would lay off 10,000 people, saving an annual $400 million in payroll, its market capitalization rose by $2 billion within a few days. Similar stories have played out hundreds of times in the past decade.

But cutting costs doesn't have to be such a bloody process. In my consulting experience over the past 13 years with more than 200 companies in varied industries, I have seen compelling evidence that a company can almost always create far more sustainable value by sensibly reducing its capital expenditures. How? Not by postponing or eliminating big spending projects, which are usually less than 20% of the budget anyway, but by conducting a rigorous, disciplined evaluation of the small-ticket items that usually get rubber-stamped. Those "little" requests often prove to be unnecessary—in some cases they duplicate other requests—or gold plated. But few managers have the time, energy, or inclination to ask about them. They should.

A solid evaluation of small-ticket capital budget items is straightforward. It involves a series of only eight questions, and the payoff is enormous. Cutting the capital budget increases cash flow dramatically, which can have an enormous impact on a company's value in the marketplace. In fact, according to my research, a permanent 15% cut in the planned level of capital spending could boost some companies' market capitalizations by as much as 30%. Better still, the company gets to keep the heads—make that brains—that might have been fired. Paying more attention to small items in the capital budget creates that business rarity—a win-win situation. (For more on the advantages of cutting capital spending, see the table "Capex Dollars Versus Job Dollars.")

When did you last go to the trouble of asking these questions about a decision involving less than $5 million?

But the eight questions don't get asked all at once. They should come in three distinct phases:

- Put the first three to your operating managers as they assemble their capital project requests. The questions will help them submit airtight proposals.

- Put the next three to yourself and your colleagues as you examine the small-ticket proposals. The

Capex Dollars Versus Job Dollars

You get more bang for the buck—or perhaps more buck for the bang—by cutting capex dollars than by cutting payroll. According to my estimates, the increased market valuation that resulted from Kodak's $400 million payroll cuts could have been achieved by a $280 million reduction in capital spending. The reason for the difference, of course, is that a company has to make severance payments—$600 million in Kodak's case—to people it has laid off. (There is no severance pay for capital.) The table compares recent payroll savings at Kodak and several other corporations with my estimated value-equivalent capex cuts.

	Kodak	Hasbro	Whirlpool	Motorola	Nike	Goodyear	DuPont
Date	Sept. 1997	Dec. 1997	Dec. 1997	June 1998	July 1998	April 1999	June 1999
Layoffs (people)	10,000	2,500	4,700	14,000	1,600	2,600	1,400
Savings per year from layoffs, in millions	$400	$50	$162	$840	$300	$100	$90
Value-equivalent annual capex cut, in millions	$280	$30	$105	$538	$68	$72	$69
Capex cut as percentage of total capex	14.5%	20.6%	23.7%	22.5%	15.1%	10.3%	3.1%

Source: Compustat, Wall Street Journal, Monitor Group analysis.

questions will help you root out much of the gold plating and redundancy built into budget requests.

- Pose the last two questions at the end of the process. They will help you improve it for the next time.

In the following pages, we'll look in detail at each phase and its questions. None of the questions, to be sure, will sound wildly unfamiliar. But when did you *Senior managers end up rubber-stamping the small proposals that often make up 80% of the capital budget.* last go to the trouble of asking such questions about a decision involving less than $5 million? The answer may be "Never," which likely means you've been spending more than you should have.

Why Small Requests Go Wrong

Before we look at the questions, it's useful to understand why small-item budget requests are often such a source of waste. The root of the problem is that senior managers with very limited time at their disposal usually feel they can best serve the company by focusing on big-ticket investments. That's not to say that focusing on big-ticket items is wrong—those investments often have huge strategic importance—but one result is that senior managers end up rubber-stamping the small proposals that often make up the remaining 80% of the capital budget.

Rubber-stamping, however, causes problems because the people preparing small-item capital spending proposals typically lack the experience or knowledge to think them through properly. And for a variety of reasons, unit managers will almost inevitably ask for more money than they need. Those reasons can be all too human. Many of the people who generate small-item spending requests are engineers. With the best intentions, engineers often indulge in gold plating. That's a natural by-product of their sensibilities—engineers generally value reliability, redundancy, and technical bells and whistles. Given a choice, they will include top-of-the-line supplies and equipment in their projects.

But it's not just engineers. Anyone at a middle or low level in an organization is likely to be risk averse, which causes overspending. No frontline manager wants to be blamed for having ordered too few spare parts when a crucial piece of machinery breaks down and creates a product shortage. Overspending may also result from unit managers' attempts to protect their turf—a low budget request this year may lead to the unit being short-changed the next.

Finally, a lot of overspending on small items is the result of a perfectly understandable dynamic. Managers on the front line have a natural tendency—even a duty—to focus on their own units' needs rather than on whether their requests overlap with those of other units. And as we'll see, some duplication may be a consequence of processes and measures put in place by senior managers. In such cases, senior managers who fail to keep an eye on small-item capital spending have only themselves to blame.

Let's turn to what senior managers can do to root out the waste—the eight questions they can ask during the budgeting cycle. First, let's examine the three questions that can help get the budget process off to a better start. (For a visual explanation of the questions, see the exhibit "Bringing Discipline to Capital Budgets at AnyCorp.")

Bringing Discipline to Capital Budgets at AnyCorp

Eight questions and a postmortem can help senior executives conduct a solid evaluation of small-ticket capital budget items. Cutting the budget increases cash flow, which can have a huge impact on a company's value in the marketplace.

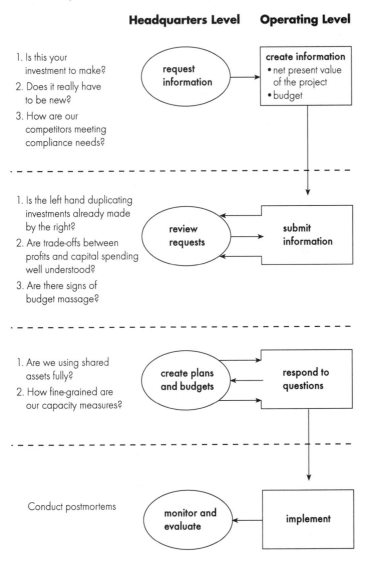

Headquarters Level   **Operating Level**

1. Is this your investment to make?
2. Does it really have to be new?
3. How are our competitors meeting compliance needs?

request information

create information
• net present value of the project
• budget

1. Is the left hand duplicating investments already made by the right?
2. Are trade-offs between profits and capital spending well understood?
3. Are there signs of budget massage?

review requests

submit information

1. Are we using shared assets fully?
2. How fine-grained are our capacity measures?

create plans and budgets

respond to questions

Conduct postmortems

monitor and evaluate

implement

Requesting the Right Information

As all Bostonians know, there's no one right way to make New England clam chowder. But whatever the details of the recipe, cooks will always need clams, milk, and potatoes. It's much the same with capital spending. There are three questions that should always be part of the mix when unit managers are cooking up a proposal:

Is this your investment to make? Sometimes a unit manager will overstep the boundaries of his control and put in a request for an investment that is the responsibility of someone else in the company—or even of some other organization altogether. That happened at one manufacturer: the sales and marketing group had requested money to buy shares in the company's dealers. The dealers, according to the sales and marketing people, would use the capital to upgrade their facilities and infrastructure. "If you must assist your dealers in upgrading their facilities," I said to the company's managers, "why not provide a financing program for them instead? After all, the storefronts are theirs, not yours." By forcing unit managers to explain why they, rather than others, need to make particular investments, senior managers can head off a lot of unnecessary spending.

Does it really have to be new? If they could afford it, most people would like to drive a new car. Managers are no different. They instinctively justify buying new machines on the grounds that the old ones need a lot of maintenance. But in my experience, that argument is deeply flawed. Equipment manufacturers in one industry I've studied, for example, routinely spend millions of dollars on new machines years earlier than they need to. In most cases, the overall cost (including the cost of breakdowns) is 30% to 40% lower if a company continues servicing an existing machine for five more years instead of buying a new one. In order to fight impulsive acquisitions of new machinery, companies should require unit managers to run the numbers on all alternative investment options open to them—including maintaining the existing assets or buying used ones. Time after time, managers will go no further than an analysis of the economics of purchasing the new machine. But even if those economics are sound, there's usually a cheaper alternative to buying new.

How are our competitors meeting compliance needs? Managers who must make investments to comply with environmental, health, and safety regulations tend to be afraid they'll be blamed for underspending if something goes wrong. This sometimes irrational fear prevents them from thinking as clearly or imaginatively as they should about how to save money on compliance, so they gold plate their investment requests. But a company should plan such expenses with the same rigor it brings to its tax obligations. A good way to combat conservative and costly compliance is to require unit managers to compare their proposals with the practices of other companies.

Reviewing the Budget Proposals

Although senior managers can avoid a lot of misspending by getting people to submit the right kind of proposals, some padding invariably gets through. Asking the following three questions during the proposal review helps uncover the fat:

Is the left hand duplicating investments already made by the right? Banks, telephone companies, and other big, far-flung organizations with complicated operations have a tendency to accumulate excess capacity. That's because many different groups of people are involved in the planning and implementation of capital expenditures. The scale of the problem can be impressive. A certain network company, for example, discovered in the course of a spending review that it had inadvertently created a 70% excess capacity in its server network. The company's field engineers, unaware that the people designing the network had built in a 30% extra server capacity, installed so many additional servers to ensure availability that excess capacity was more than doubled. In order to expose this kind of unnecessary spending, managers need to check how well the various decision-makers involved with a particular item are communicating with one another as they pass the item down the line. If there's no regular, honest exchange of information, there's a high chance the company is spending a lot on unnecessary capacity.

Are the trade-offs between profits and capital spending well understood? In some companies, no amount of prior consideration will stop managers from sending in requests for new assets. In such cases, it usually turns out that the company suffers from a financial culture that places earnings above all other performance measures. Take the example of a certain telecommunications company. Its network designers insisted on using extra thick telegraph poles and specified that they be placed five feet closer together than required by law. Such a distribution system, they declared, would be better able to withstand falling tree limbs during storms. Asked why the company didn't trim the trees instead, the engineers replied that the cost of trimming would reduce the company's profitability, while the extra capital investment would not, since it wouldn't appear in the earnings statement! Our analysis, which capitalized the after-tax cost of the extra annual maintenance so that it could be compared with the capital cost of the distribution system, showed that the stronger distribution system was several times more expensive.

Are there signs of budget massage? Budget massaging is common at large companies where senior managers don't police capital spending beyond looking to see whether a unit's spending matches its forecasts. In such companies, unit managers may be reluctant to propose reductions in their capital spending because they are afraid the head office won't be generous when they need an increase; on the other hand, they may be afraid that asking for too much money will provoke a close encounter with the company's internal auditors. So they may attempt to massage the budget in a couple of ways. One is to shuffle expenditures between capital and annual operating budgets so that the capital budget never shows a dramatic change from year to year. Another is to practice year-end loading—when managers realize they're going to underspend the allocations they've requested, they start putting in unnecessary expenses to make up the shortfall. A dented fender, for example, becomes an excuse to request a new pickup truck. By going to the trouble during the year to query unit managers about small decisions of this sort, senior managers can discourage units from massaging their budgets.

Revisit Business Processes

After the unit managers have gone off to spend their money, senior managers should look again at the procedures that have been set up to improve the efficiency of the company's spending and make sure they are working. The next two questions can uncover many problems:

Are we using shared assets fully? At networked businesses that use a lot of shared assets—car-rental companies, airlines, electric utilities, telecoms, Internet service providers, and the like—spending is highly sensitive to slow-moving bureaucratic procedures. A certain telecommunications company, for example, was investing millions in new servers, even though its network wasn't growing quickly enough to justify the new equipment. The reason, it turned out, was that the official procedure for disconnecting and relocating unneeded servers took so long that they didn't show up as excess on capacity lists until the year after they were deemed unnecessary. The best way for a senior manager to find out if this sort of thing is going on is to check the extent to which shared assets are really being utilized— and not just by looking at extra-capacity lists. If shared assets are not fully utilized most of the time, it's likely you will have to revisit your company's paper trails.

At one cable company, a cable could be classified as fully utilized if only three of its 33 fibers were lit.

How fine-grained are our capacity measures? Not all bureaucracy-induced overspending is a result of slow procedures. Sometimes, overspending is a direct consequence of a company's measures for recognizing that it needs more investment in equipment. If such measures aren't adequately fine-grained, managers can underestimate the capacity of equipment or networks. This happened at a cable company whose capacity measures indicated that a bundle of optical fibers was being fully used if just one fiber was carrying information. But each bundle consisted of 11 fibers; since there were three bundles per cable, a line with 33 fibers could be classified as fully utilized if as few as three fibers were lit. Naturally, the company installed far more cable than it needed.

Conducting a Postmortem

When all is said and done, even the most careful budgeting process is fallible. What's more, in a fast-paced marketplace like the Internet you can lose out by taking time to probe deeply as you make decisions on capital spending. That's why managers need to supplement budget supervision with regular audits of units' capital spending. There are three rules to follow in conducting such inquiries:

BE INCLUSIVE

Many companies leave their audits to people in the finance department, who often confront workers in an adversarial manner. That's wrong. Audit teams should always include employees from the departments being reviewed. For a company to unearth the kind of overspending I've been talking about, it's essential that the people who know most about the operations buy into the process. At the same time, the team needs to have some organizational authority. It is, after all, going to be asking embarrassing questions. The team should therefore report to a senior executive who has the muscle to clear obstacles from its path and make any changes it may recommend.

HAVE A CLEAR GOAL

The audit team should not only identify what went wrong with last year's budget, it should come up with recommendations for change. A good audit should specify ways to save at least 10% of a unit's capital budget. If senior managers want to stretch a team, however, they should set a higher goal of 15% or 20%.

GROUP SMALL ITEMS TOGETHER

The really big savings come when senior managers discover systematic problems with whole classes of expenditures. It's easier to find such problems if you look at all the requests for particular items—transformers at an electric utility or clamps on a pipeline, for example—at the same time. I remember an executive of a chemical company—he was blind—who had his staff construct a detailed scale model of a new chemical plant; having reviewed the design in three dimensions, he reduced the cost of the plant 10% by rerouting pipes to save on expensive elbow joints.

A GOOD AUDIT CAN TURN UP surprising horrors. One of my favorite stories is about a telecommunications company I was advising eight years ago. In the course of reviewing the company's capital spending, I came across an internal rule specifying that all cables be laid at a depth of two meters. I asked the head of engineering about it, and he said that at two meters, the cable network would be protected against a thermonuclear magnetic impulse created by the explosion of a hydrogen bomb. "Fair enough," I replied, "but what happens to your customers when the bomb goes off?" The company saved $80 million a year by reducing its cable depth to one meter. If you make the eight questions and an audit a part of your company's small-item capital budgeting process, you may well find a lot of buried treasure.

Originally published in September–October 2000
Reprint R00503

We Don't Need Another Hero

JOSEPH L. BADARACCO, JR.

Executive Summary

EVERYBODY LOVES THE STORIES of heroes like Martin Luther King, Jr., Mother Teresa, and Gandhi. But the heroic model of moral leadership usually doesn't work in the corporate world. Modesty and restraint are largely responsible for the achievements of the most effective moral leaders in business.

The author, a specialist in business ethics, says the quiet leaders he has studied follow four basic rules in meeting ethical challenges and making decisions. The rules constitute an important resource for executives who want to encourage the development of such leaders among their middle managers.

The first rule is "Put things off till tomorrow." The passage of time allows turbulent waters to calm and lets leaders' moral instincts emerge. "Pick your battles" means that quiet leaders don't waste political capital on fights they can't win; they save it for occasions when they really want to fight. "Bend the rules, don't break them" sounds easier than it is—bending the rules in order to resolve a complicated situation requires imagination, discipline, restraint, flexibility, and entrepreneurship. The fourth rule, "Find a compromise," reflects the author's finding that quiet leaders try not to see situations as polarized tests of ethical principles. These individuals work hard to craft compromises that are "good enough"— responsible and workable enough—to satisfy themselves, their companies, and their customers.

The vast majority of difficult problems are solved through the consistent striving of people working far from the limelight. Their quiet approach to leadership doesn't inspire, thrill, or provide story lines for uplifting TV shows. But the unglamorous efforts of quiet leaders make a tremendous difference every day in the corporate world.

E VERYBODY LOVES THE STORIES of great leaders, especially great moral leaders. Think of Martin Luther King, Jr., Mother Teresa, and Gandhi. We exalt these individuals as role models and celebrate their achievements. They represent, we proclaim, the gold standard of ethical behavior.

Or do they? I don't ask this because I question the value of ethical behavior—far from it. I ask because over the course of my career as a specialist in business ethics, I have observed that the most effective moral leaders in the corporate world often sever the connection between morality and public heroism. These men and women aren't high-profile champions of right over wrong and don't want to be. They don't spearhead large-scale ethical crusades. They move patiently, carefully, and incrementally. They right—or prevent—moral wrongs in the workplace inconspicuously and usually without casualties. I have come to call these people quiet leaders because their modesty and restraint are in large measure responsible for their extraordinary achievements. And since many big problems can only be resolved by a long series of small efforts, quiet leadership, despite its seemingly slow pace, often turns out to be the quickest way to make the corporation—and the world—a better place.

In this article, I explore the findings of my four-year effort to understand how quiet leaders see themselves, think about ethical problems, and make effective decisions. Although all names have been changed, the anecdotes below are based on more than 150 case studies that I gathered from several sources, including direct observation, participation in situations as an adviser, and papers and accounts by many of my older MBA students who came from corporate positions with serious management responsibilities. The stories have convinced me that while certain ethical challenges require direct, public action, quiet leadership is the best way to do the right thing in many cases. That's because quiet leadership is practical, effective, and sustainable. Quiet leaders prefer to pick their battles and fight them carefully rather than go down in a blaze of glory for a single, dramatic effort.

Two Ethical Approaches

To understand why quiet moral leadership works so well, consider what can result from a public display of heroism. Rebecca Waide was a manager at a small regional bank. Convinced that a set of lending policies was exploitative, she made an appointment with her boss and quickly launched into a made-for-Hollywood speech about the rights of the poor. "I can almost swear that while I was talking, there was inspirational music in the background," she says. "I must have sounded like Sally Field in *Norma Rae*. I wanted to defend the oppressed."

It didn't work. Waide's emotionalism and lack of careful preparation undermined her credibility. The company thought its policies were sound, particularly for riskier customers, and her boss didn't appreciate the lecture. Not surprisingly, the company's lending policies remained unchanged.

Now consider Barry Nelan, another banker whose case I studied. He was going through files one day when he discovered that a company had been charged too little interest on a bank loan for more than five years. He wondered if the bank's executives, some of whom were good friends with the borrower's managers, knew about the problem but were conveniently overlooking it. He feared that his boss, who had authorized the loan, might be scapegoated if the problem came to the attention of others.

At first, Nelan saw only two choices. He could report the error through official channels and let the chips fall where they might, or he could leave things alone. But then he came up with an alternative: He took the matter directly to his boss. His boss's first instinct was to rebury the problem, but Nelan said that if they couldn't find an answer, he would be forced to inform bank executives about the mistake. They sat down with the client and restructured the loan, then reported the problem and the solution to the executives. Nelan was careful, patient, and politically astute throughout the process. He managed to benefit himself and the organization while protecting his colleague's job. He was the quintessential quiet leader.

Operating Instructions

My research suggests that quiet moral leaders follow four basic rules in meeting ethical challenges and making decisions. Although not always used together, the rules constitute an indispensable tool kit that can help quiet leaders work out the dilemmas they face. Some tactics may seem a little too clever or even ethically dubious. Certainly, few people would want to work at jobs where such moves constitute business as usual. Nevertheless, these guidelines often prove critical when leaders have real responsibilities to meet.

The rules serve another purpose, too. By offering insight into how an organization's unknown soldiers achieve their moral victories, the guidelines can help top executives foster the development of quiet leaders among middle managers. Tactics they can use include setting examples of quiet leadership in meetings; going out of the way to praise and reward individuals who take quiet, sustained, effective approaches to problems; and appointing top managers who are themselves quiet leaders. Such actions send powerful messages about the right way to deal with difficult, messy problems.

PUT THINGS OFF TILL TOMORROW

When ethical dilemmas heat up, quiet leaders often look for ways to buy time. Careful execution of this tactic can spell the difference between success and failure. The passage of time allows turbulent waters to calm. It also lets leaders analyze the subtle ways in which individuals and events interact—it lets them look for patterns and watch for opportunities to arise from the flow of events. More important, sound moral instincts have a chance to emerge. Of course, there are situations—such as when a defective product is about to be shipped or a misleading financial report is about to be released—that call for immediate action. But the drama of do-or-die situations can lead us to exaggerate the frequency with which they arise. The vast majority of practical ethical challenges facing most managers are mundane and subtle, calling for the unglamorous virtues of patience and staying power.

To see how quiet leaders create buffer zones that permit them to put their unglamorous virtues to use, let's look at a quiet leader who succeeded in thinking clearly and moving at a deliberate pace, even though top management was breathing down his neck. Kyle Williams had recently become a branch president for a small regional bank in Maine. He was excited about a job that gave him visibility and profit-and-loss responsibility. The only drawback to the promotion was the intense financial pressure on the bank and its senior executives. Williams was told that if the stock price didn't rise quickly, the bank was likely to be bought and dismantled by a larger bank.

Among the 55 employees Williams inherited were four chronic underperformers, including a 56-year-old teller who was notoriously rude to customers and raised the issue of age discrimination whenever her performance was questioned. Another of the four was a widow who had been at the bank 30 years. She was recovering from cancer surgery but was reluctant to go on disability. Finally, there were the two lead loan officers: One lacked initiative and imagination; he did everything by the book. The other had more potential, but even the promise of a performance bonus didn't fire her up.

Williams was eager to reduce expenses, but he wanted to avoid shortsighted cost-cutting measures and to be fair to longtime employees. He thought firing the four underperformers, as was tacitly but clearly expected of him, might embroil the company in legal problems. He needed time to persuade his boss to take a different approach, such as transferring the underperformers or encouraging them to take early retirement. If there had been less stress on the bank, Williams would have openly argued for moving slowly. But given the pressures, a request for more time could have prompted the bank management to replace him with someone willing to clean house more quickly. So he took steps to divert attention while he postponed action. Call it game playing if you will, but Williams's games were hardly trivial amusements. They were tactics that allowed him to find a "good enough" solution to the bank's problems.

There are two kinds of time buying: quick fixes and strategic stalling. Everyday dodges such as, "I've got someone on the other line—can I get back to you on that?" can buy a few hours or a couple of days; such gambits have helped countless managers whose backs were against the wall. But Williams needed weeks to rectify the situation he inherited. His situation called for strategic stalling.

The fundamental line of attack in strategic stalling is to dot all the i's and cross all the t's. As a first step, Williams tossed his boss a bone by cutting a few unnecessary expenses (badly managed operations often have plenty of those). He then sought legal advice on his personnel issues—after all, one employee had already raised the issue of age discrimination. He also got human resources involved, a move that gained him weeks. Then he began

Before they take stands or tackle tough problems, quiet leaders calculate how much political capital they are putting at risk and what they can expect in return.

to raise strategic questions: Do we have the appropriate contingency plans in place? Are there more options we should evaluate?

Strategic stalling gave Williams time to resolve all the issues he faced. He never caught the teller being rude, but he fired her for leaving large amounts of cash unattended. The widow went on permanent disability. After pep talks, quotas, and incentives failed to motivate the two loan officers, Williams threatened to fire them. One quit; the other, galvanized into action, became a first-rate loan officer.

PICK YOUR BATTLES

Political capital is the hard currency of organizational life. You earn it by establishing a reputation for getting things done and by having a network of people who can appreciate and reward your efforts. Political capital is hard to accumulate and devilishly easy to dissipate. That's why quiet leaders invest it astutely and use it with care. Before they take stands or tackle tough problems, quiet leaders calculate how much political capital they are putting at risk and what they can expect in return. In other words, they pick their battles wisely.

For an example of how not to squander political capital, consider Michele Petryni, the public relations manager at a large Washington, DC, law firm. Petryni stood in astonishment one day as she was refused admittance to a meeting with several law partners. The purpose of the meeting was to deal with a very sensitive problem in the firm, and for several weeks Petryni had been working with one of the partners on a solution. Now the partner was telling her that a "nonpartner female" would stir up the brew.

Petryni was shocked and furious. Her first impulse was to threaten a discrimination lawsuit. But Petryni was also shrewd. She understood that most of the time, getting on a white horse and leading a charge does little good. If she forced her way into the meeting, no one would be openly sympathetic and a few partners would be overtly hostile. Besides, she liked her job. She had been promoted rapidly and was widely respected in the firm. She didn't want to be labeled a troublemaker. So Petryni decided not to waste her hard-earned political capital. She opted for pointed humor instead.

"You know," she said to the partner she had been working with, "I've never been told I couldn't play ball because I didn't have the right equipment!" He appreciated her effort to smooth over the rupture and later told the senior partner what happened.

Instead of acting like moral bookkeepers, quiet leaders bend the rules and own up to their deeper responsibilities.

The senior partner sought out Petryni and apologized for the firm. He acknowledged there were sexists in the firm but said they were an aging minority. He asked Petryni for her patience and support.

How well did Petryni handle this situation? Her tactics didn't fit the standard model of heroic leadership. She didn't tell the first partner that he was doing something obnoxious, insulting, and perhaps illegal. She didn't go to the meeting, even though she belonged there. Many people would argue that she surrendered her interests. But Petryni made a prudent investment. Her restrained approach enabled her to make her case to the partner she had worked with and the senior partner without offending either. Of course, her efforts didn't change the firm's culture, but she was able to get management to acknowledge that there was a problem. Most important, Petryni added untold riches to her political capital for the occasions when she really wants to fight.

BEND THE RULES, DON'T BREAK THEM

Most of us don't associate bending the rules with moral leadership. But following the rules can be a moral cop-out. If a friend asks if you like her new shoes, and you think they look ridiculous, you don't tell the truth. And when the Gestapo demanded to know who was hiding Jews, some people lied. Between the trivial and the tragic are many everyday situations in which responsible people work hard to find ways to maneuver within the boundaries set by the rules. Instead of acting like moral bookkeepers, they bend the rules and own up to their deeper responsibilities.

Consider Jonathan Balint, a consultant who was working on a large project for a manufacturing company. Balint's brother-in-law happened to work for the client and was trying to decide whether to take an offer from another company or stay in his present job. Balint had learned that the client was three weeks away from announcing a major layoff; Balint's brother-in-law would likely lose his job. Should Balint tip him off to the danger of staying at the company?

Balint didn't want to betray the confidentiality of his client or his firm; doing so, he knew, would be wrong, and it could severely hurt his career. So he spent several days searching for wiggle room. He took the rules seriously but didn't treat them as a paint-by-numbers exercise. Eventually he decided he could send signals to his brother-in-law without revealing everything he knew.

For example, he reminded him that no one is indispensable, that anyone can be laid off; Balint also said he had heard rumors about impending layoffs at local manufacturers. His brother-in-law took the hint.

Balint's choice perfectly illustrates the way quiet leaders work. They know that breaking the rules is wrong—and in some cases illegal. They also want to protect their reputations, networks, and career prospects. So they don't break the rules. But when situations are complicated, they typically search for ways to bend the rules imaginatively. Quiet leaders don't view such tactics as ideal ways to handle problems, but sometimes situations give them no choice. Balint, for example, had competing obligations to his client and his family. In complex ethical situations such as these, bending the rules is never easy and certainly not fun. Indeed, bending the rules—as opposed to breaking them—is hard work. It requires imagination, discipline, and restraint, along with flexibility and entrepreneurship.

FIND A COMPROMISE

Compromise has a bad reputation in some circles. For some people, compromise is what politicians and lobbyists do in smoke-filled rooms. Many of us believe that good people—moral people—refuse to compromise. They tell the truth, the whole truth, and nothing but the truth, and they are always fair. Quiet leaders understand this view of moral principles, but they don't find it particularly useful in most situations. They reject the idea that moral principles can be treated like salami and sacrificed slice by slice, but they try not to see situations as black-and-white tests of ethical principles. For this reason, crafting responsible, workable compromises is not just something that quiet leaders occasionally do. It defines who they are.

Take Roger Darco, for example. Darco was a hard-working, successful sales rep who learned he wouldn't be able to sell a longtime customer a new server it needed. The servers were in limited supply, and his company was saving them for "premier" customers. Roger raised the issue with his boss and got lots of sympathy—but no assistance. Instead, his boss reminded him of the importance of making quota.

On the face of it, Darco had only two options. He could refuse to give his client the server, or he could violate company policy and sell the server by faking documents, as some reps were doing. But somewhere between extremes there is often a compromise solution. Darco found it by discovering that if his client was willing to be a test site, it could get the server early. The client agreed and got the machine it needed.

Darco may not look like much of a moral hero, but he did take on a complicated ethical issue and get it right. He didn't start a revolution—the situation didn't call for a revolution. Yet by finding a workable compromise, Darco uncovered a middle that was "good enough"— responsible enough and workable enough—to satisfy his customer, his company, and himself.

The Silence Between the Waves

The quiet approach to leadership is easy to misunderstand and mock. It doesn't inspire or thrill. It focuses on small things, careful moves, controlled and measured efforts. It doesn't provide story lines for uplifting TV shows. In contrast to heroic leadership, quiet leadership doesn't show us the heights that the human spirit can reach. What, then, do the imperfect, unglamorous, every-day efforts of quiet leaders amount to? Almost every-thing. The vast majority of difficult human problems are not solved by the dramatic efforts of people at the top but by the consistent striving of people working far from the limelight.

This was the view of Albert Schweitzer, a hero if ever there was one. After he won the 1952 Nobel Peace Prize for working with the poor in central Africa, Schweitzer used the money to build a facility for treating leprosy. He changed many lives and inspired countless others. Yet he was unromantic about the role of great moral heroes in shaping the world: "Of all the will toward the ideal in mankind only a small part can manifest itself in public action," he wrote. "All the rest of this force must be content with small and obscure deeds. The sum of these, however, is a thousand times stronger than the acts of those who receive wide public recognition. The latter, compared to the former, are like the foam on the waves of a deep ocean."

Ordinary People

THE QUIET MORAL LEADERS in my study typically work in the middle of organizations where they look for modest but effective solutions to the problems they face. They don't aspire to perfection. In fact, their thinking is distinguished by two characteristics that would almost certainly disqualify them for sainthood: Their motivations are decidedly mixed, and their worldviews are unabashedly realistic. Let's take a closer look at each of these traits.

Mixed Motives

According to the heroic model of moral leadership, true leaders make great sacrifices for the benefit of others. In truth, however, very few people would sacrifice their lives for a cause (which is why we revere the handful of people who do and why we call them saints and heroes). Most people, most of the time, act out of mixed and complex motives. They want to help others, but they also care about themselves. They have lives, interests, and commitments that they are unwilling to risk. Because they need to put food on the table, crusades and martyrdom are not options.

Consider John Ayer, an experienced sales rep at a major pharmaceutical company that had been selling physicians a very popular drug for treating depression. Although federal laws forbade it, the company started discreetly promoting the drug to doctors whose patients wanted to lose weight or stop smoking. Ayer didn't want to limit his pay or promotion prospects, but he didn't want to break the law or contribute to patients suffering side effects from unapproved uses. So he tried to walk a fine line: He talked about unapproved uses of the drug only if doctors asked him. But as more and more of his sales came from those uses, he became increasingly troubled and decided to stop answering questions about unapproved uses. He also visited doctors who were prescribing the drug for problems other than depression and discussed the risks and side effects with them. Then he went a step further: He told his manager and a few other sales reps what he was doing and why, in part to protect himself against future liability.

By any standard of moral purity, Ayer doesn't measure up very well. His motives for doing the right thing are unmistakably self-serving. As he puts it: "My decision was made as much out of fear as anything else. I was scared of finding out that a patient had died because one of my clients had prescribed the drug at a high dose. I also suspected that my company would not stand behind me if something horrible happened."

Although Ayer's motives were hardly unadulterated, they nonetheless gave him the strength to persevere. Indeed, when there is a tough moral challenge, the degree of a person's motivation can matter more than the purity of the motives. That's because real leaders draw strength from a multitude of motives—high and low, conscious and unconscious, altruistic and self-serving. The challenge is not to suppress self-interest or low motives but to harness, channel, and direct them. If Ayer had been motivated by empathy alone, I believe he would have been far less likely to act.

Of course, mixed motives can leave people in Ayer's position feeling bewildered and frustrated, but that's not all bad. Confusion in complex situations can prompt people to pause, look around, reflect, and learn before they plunge into action. Soldiers who clear minefields move slowly and methodically, but their deliberate pace takes nothing away from their valor and adds greatly to their effectiveness. Indeed, my research shows that when quiet leaders succeed, it is usually *because* of their complicated and ambivalent motives, not despite them.

Clinging to Reality

Ayer's quiet approach to leadership raises important questions. Should he have done more? Should he have taken the issue to senior management? Should he have blown the whistle and alerted federal regulators?

I believe the answer is no. All too often, whistle-blowing is career suicide. Torpedoing your career might be fine if you end up changing your company—or the world—for the better. But dramatic action seldom leads to such impressive results. Quiet leaders pay close attention to the limits of their power. They don't overestimate how much influence they have over other people or how well they can control events in an uncertain world. Each quiet leader realizes that, in most situations, he or she is only one piece on a chessboard.

Such realism is often confused with cynicism. But realists aren't cynics; they merely see things in Technicolor, whereas cynics see black and white. Quiet leaders' expansive vision of reality in all its colors helps them avoid acts of heroic self-immolation.

Consider Ben Waterhouse, the head of marketing at a medium-sized company. His boss asked him to drop a high-performing ad firm and replace it with a six-month-old agency. Waterhouse was flabbergasted, especially when he discovered that the owner of the new agency was a good friend of his boss. Waterhouse's immediate instinct was to dash off a strong memo or call a meeting with his boss's superior. But after he calmed down, Waterhouse recognized that he didn't have the clout to override his boss on this issue. So he developed a pragmatic plan. He gave the new ad agency a couple of very challenging assignments, which they handled poorly. He documented the failures to his boss, who opted to stick with the veteran agency.

From the perspective of heroism, Waterhouse's story seems more like a cop-out than a profile in courage. He didn't take a stand on principle; in fact, he engaged in subterfuge. But Waterhouse's realism was not a moral handicap—far from it. It gave him a sense of proportion and a degree of modesty and caution that helped him move wisely across a hazardous landscape. In the process, he managed to preserve one of the company's most valued relationships. He also kept his company from incurring unnecessary expenses. This made much more sense—realistically and ethically—than flaming out in a single heroic, but futile, act.

TAKEN TOGETHER, THE TRAITS OF mixed motives and hard-boiled realism describe the working assumptions of quiet moral leaders. A moral compass points these individuals in the right direction, but the guidelines for quiet leadership help them get to their destinations—in one piece.

Originally published in September 2001
Reprint R0108H

Patching

Restitching Business Portfolios in Dynamic Markets

KATHLEEN M. EISENHARDT AND
SHONA L. BROWN

Executive Summary

IN TURBULENT MARKETS, businesses and opportunities
are constantly falling out of alignment. New technologies
and emerging markets create fresh opportunities. Converging markets produce more. And of course, some
markets fade. In this landscape of continuous flux, it's
more important to build corporate-level strategic processes that enable dynamic repositioning than it is to build
any particular defensible position.

That's why smart corporate strategists use *patching*, a
process of mapping and remapping business units to create a shifting mix of highly focused, tightly aligned businesses that can respond to changing market opportunities. Patching is not just another name for reorganizing;
patchers have a distinctive mindset. Traditional managers
see structure as stable; patching managers believe structure is inherently temporary. Traditional managers set

corporate strategy first, but patching managers keep the organization focused on the right set of business opportunities and let strategy emerge from individual businesses.

Although the focus of patching is flexibility, the process itself follows a pattern. Patching changes are usually small in scale and made frequently. Patching should be done quickly; the emphasis is on getting the patch about right and fixing problems later. Patches should have a test drive before they're formalized but then be tightly scripted after they've been announced. And patching won't work without the right infrastructure: modular business units, fine-grained and complete unit-level metrics, and companywide compensation parity. The authors illustrate how patching works and point out some common stumbling blocks.

In 1984, MANAGERS AT Hewlett-Packard's Boise, Idaho, outpost launched a fledgling business based on laser technology for computer printing applications. They anticipated initial unit sales of 10,000 per month; they achieved 100,000 shortly after launch. By the end of the decade, HP's managers had catapulted their Boise start-up into a $5 billion growth engine that was driven not just by one printer technology but by three. Today the printing business extends into digital photography, wireless information distribution, and e-commerce imaging. It continues to drive corporate growth.

Their secret? HP's managers relied on a corporate-level process we call *patching* to create a continually shifting mix of highly focused, tightly aligned businesses that could respond to changing market opportunities.[1] In the case of laser-jet printing, the executives lopped off pieces of the core business to form new businesses like networked printers, keeping the laser-jet managers focused on their booming business. They launched businesses in related products like scanners and faxes. They transferred businesses from one division to another to make better use of skills and to optimize scale. They combined businesses to create critical mass and increase cash flow in order to drive new growth. Most significant, Hewlett-Packard's managers relied on patching to develop a second printer business built around ink-jet technology, and later used patching to revitalize their Wintel and UNIX computer businesses. Today these businesses represent roughly 80% of the company's revenues.

Patching is the strategic process by which corporate executives routinely remap businesses to changing market opportunities. It can take the form of adding, splitting, transferring, exiting, or combining chunks of businesses. Patching is less critical when markets are relatively unchanging, but when markets are turbulent, patching becomes crucial. It allows corporate managers to focus on the best opportunities and leave the less promising ones behind. By dynamically adjusting businesses to match changing market opportunities, managers are more likely to focus on high-potential businesses, to uncover the profit levers that drive effective strategy in those businesses, and to create economic value for the corporation.

At first glance, patching may seem to be just another name for reorganizing. But patchers have a distinctive mind-set. While managers in traditional companies see structure as mostly stable, managers in companies that patch believe structure is inherently temporary. Patchers also develop corporate strategy differently. Traditional managers set corporate strategy first, whereas managers who patch keep the organization focused on the right overall set of business opportunities and then let strategy emerge from individual businesses.

Patching changes are usually small in scale and made frequently—think evolution, not revolution. Managers at patching companies pay extraordinary attention to the size of their business units, which should be small enough for agility and large enough for efficiency. They've also learned that patching won't work without the right infrastructure: business chunks must be modular, business-unit-level metrics should be fine grained and complete, and compensation within the company needs to be consistent. Finally, they know that patching implementation follows certain principles. Patching should be done quickly. The emphasis is on getting the patch roughly right and fixing problems later. (See the exhibit "Reorganization Versus Patching.")

Hewlett-Packard is not the only corporation that has relied on patching to sustain long-term reinvention and growth. Patching is a key factor in the success of several traditionally high-performing companies like 3M and Johnson & Johnson. 3M's managers, for example, grew their highly successful microreplication operations by adding, combining, and transferring businesses around market applications as diverse as computer privacy screens and reflective guardrails. Patching is also part of the repertoire at new-economy stars like Dell Computer, Intuit, and Cisco Systems. And it's the next step in the reinvention strategy of companies like British Petroleum, AlliedSignal, and Lucent Technologies, where managers have split their traditional bureaucracies to create a patchwork of distinct businesses. For example, BP's CEO, Sir John Browne, began his turnaround of the petroleum giant by splintering the bureaucracy into 90 businesses.

Similarly, Richard McGinn reshaped Lucent's 4 sprawling businesses into 11 tightly focused ones.

Our understanding of patching emerged from almost a decade of research into the reasons behind corporate success in high-velocity, intensely competitive industries. One phase of the research took us inside 12 successful companies in different segments of the computer industry—an industry that is the prototype of this new competitive reality.

Companies that patch well can outperform the most efficient capital markets.

Reorganization Versus Patching

	Reorganization	Patching
Role of Change	Change as defensive reaction	Change as proactive weapon
Scale of Change	Changes are sweeping	Changes are mostly small, some are moderate, a few are large
Frequency	Changes are rare	Changes are ongoing
Formalization	Every change is unique	Change process is routine and follows standard patching moves
Driver of Change	Get business focus right	Get business focus and size right
Precision	Optimal restructuring at specific point in time	Roughly right realignments over time
Metrics	Collect fine-grained metrics only for infrequent reorganizations	Regularly track extensive, fine-grained metrics on modular businesses
Compensation	Not relevant	Companywide parity

We then tested the relevance of these ideas in other industries through targeted case studies.

Many management thinkers today are asking, Can the corporation add value beyond that of the sum of the businesses? The answer is yes. Managers who can quickly reconfigure resources into the right chunks at the right scale to address shifting market opportunities—in other words, managers who can patch well—can create multibusiness companies that outperform even the most efficient capital markets. Patching is a crucial, corporate-level strategic process that can build extraordinary value by dynamically stitching the quilt of businesses within the corporation. (See "The New Corporate Strategy" at the end of this article.)

Frequent, Routine, and Mostly Small Changes

Managers who patch make lots of usually small changes to their organizational structure. These patches can take several forms—splits and additions are the obvious ones, but there are also combinations, transfers, and exits.

Dell Computer regularly uses splits to focus more closely on target markets. In 1994, Dell split into two segments. The transaction segment dealt with customers who bought equipment in quantities of one or two; the relationship segment catered to customers who bought in greater quantities—in 50s, 100s, or 1,000s. By 1996, Dell's managers had split the company into six segments. Since then, Dell has announced a new split almost quarterly. Commercial relationship accounts are now segmented into corporate and small business; government accounts are split into federal, state, and local; other nonprofits are divided into segments such as education and medical. As a result, Dell's business-level managers stay tightly focused on increasingly specific market opportunities, which they can exploit in very targeted ways.

Managers at Dell's arch rival, Compaq, also patch, but they rely more on additions of new product divisions— such as storage devices and workstations—and exits— such as the company's departure from the networking business. Compaq's corporate executives keep business-level managers focused on taking well-defined product market "hills," without dictating the strategy for making it happen. Managers at Cisco Systems also frequently reshape their portfolio by adding new businesses, but they do so primarily through small acquisitions—more than 20 in the past four years. As a consequence, Cisco has transformed itself from a small networking company into a broad-based telecommunications player organized around a patchwork of very focused business units.

Bombardier is an example of a company outside the high-tech industry that relies on patching. Managers at the Canadian manufacturer of aircraft, mass transit vehicles, and other forms of transport, think in terms of frequent, small reorganizations, especially using a kind of transfer called "raising the orbit."[2] In one instance, several of Bombardier's manufacturing businesses had developed fledgling service operations. Recognizing a growth opportunity that was not central to the main strategic direction of any existing business, corporate executives pulled services into a new business. This move had two effects. It elevated services to a higher orbit of strategic prominence. It also energized and focused services managers on their opportunity. Services has since become a major new growth trajectory for the corporation.

Hewlett-Packard's managers have relied on a wider repertoire of patching maneuvers than most managers. In one move, managers combined a new networked laser-jet printer business (based on an emergent technology for an established market) with another printing business (based on an older, cash cow technology). The rationale was twofold: to transfer market knowledge from the older business to the new one and to fund the new business. In another move, managers transferred the ink-jet color business from one division to another in order to exploit the second business's innovation skills. More recently, HP's managers used another kind of transfer move. They built a "parking lot" of businesses— where the established scanner business was temporarily grouped with new businesses in Internet applications and wireless appliances. This move gave critical administrative scale to the businesses. Perhaps best known is the now legendary split of the ink-jet from the laser-jet business. Although that split was significant, it was only one of many patching moves that built HP's printing empire, which now dominates the industry worldwide. (The company's recent split into two parts, however, is more a classic reorganization than it is a patch.)

As the examples demonstrate, managers at patching companies often make the same moves again and again. Therefore, they have created routines that support the patching process. For instance, Cisco's pattern for adding businesses includes routines for selecting acquisition targets (the preference is for new companies about to launch their first product), for mobilizing special integration teams, for handling stock options, and for tracking employee retention rates. The routines also cover mundane details like when and how to change the contents of the vending machines at the acquired company.

While most patching changes are small, patchers do execute changes of all sizes. As a general rule, managers who patch make lots of small changes, occasional medium-sized ones, and a few large ones. Small moves, such as splitting the government business into state and local divisions, are the norm at Dell. But Dell's managers occasionally make a large move, such as shifting their Asian business from a country focus to a channel focus. At Cisco, too, most patching adjustments are small, but occasionally managers make a major move like the acquisition of Stratacom. All managers find large changes to be more challenging than small ones. But managers at patching companies usually execute large moves more effectively than their traditional competitors for one obvious reason: they're limber from frequent repatching while their competitors are, by comparison, out of shape.

Think of patching, then, as a series of frequent, usually small, realignments that are part of the organizational routine. Small and routine they may be, but they drive the arithmetic of shareholder value. Effective corporate managers patch to achieve optimal margins, to create focus on high-potential businesses, and ultimately to drive growth.

Size Matters

Managers who patch well constantly manage the size of their businesses. They balance on the edge of chaos between agility and efficiency. Small business units allow managers to focus on the specific demands of key customer segments and to exploit niche opportunities for growth. They also make it easy to pursue fragmenting markets, markets evolving at different rates, and businesses that need different operating models. However, units that are too small may result in inefficiencies. They may have excessive overhead, require too much coordination, and involve loss of scale economies or market power.

NovaMed Eyecare Management, a medical start-up, is a telling illustration. This high-flying venture provides top-quality eye care with cutting edge technology at a competitive price. How does it do it? One way is by carefully managing the size of the practice groups in each of its markets. A minimum number of doctors in a regional market like metro Chicago or St. Louis creates enough scale to support the professional management, information technology, ancillary services, and media access that drive efficiencies. But the number of practitioners is small enough that the doctors can make timely decisions and avoid cannibalizing one another's practices. If the practices were bigger, NovaMed could not be as selective regarding doctor quality. Being bigger would also create unhealthy competition for patients, confuse relationships with referring providers like optometrists, and lose the local character of health care. If the practices were too small, overhead expenses would damage profitability and inhibit physician specialization. NovaMed executives arrive at the optimal patch size by carefully segmenting markets based on specific geographic and operating parameters. Senior management readjusts the scale as changes such as new surgical procedures open up fresh market opportunities.

While managing patch size is important for new ventures like NovaMed, it can be crucial for big corporations trying to respond with agility in dynamic markets. Microsoft is a good example. Although the company itself is a software giant, Microsoft executives try to keep their applications businesses at or below 200 people so that managers can develop an in-depth understanding of their business and motivate people—particularly their star developers—effectively. Having bigger business units would make it possible to develop larger, more complex software programs, but it would lower motivation by distancing developers from their product and so ultimately hurt the business. Conversely, having patches that were too small would not give Microsoft the programming scale needed to write substantial software applications.

Small patches can indeed be a problem. Consider the example of a major telecommunications company that was configured into many small, independent divisions. When faced with significant opportunities in the emerging wireless communications sector, none of the divisions had the technical or financial resources to go it alone. At the urging of senior management, five divisional managers tried to coordinate their attempts to enter the new market. But because the units were organizationally distinct, together their cost structure was higher than the competition's. Furthermore, despite good intentions, managers became swamped in endless meetings and constant bickering—coordinating five different points of view was just too challenging. The collaboration was a failure, even though the company had several world-class technologies and ample financial resources. Stitching together several divisions into a larger patch or raising the orbit of the

In volatile markets, corporate strategy should focus on processes more than on positioning.

wireless pieces into their own patch would have lowered operating overhead, built a critical mass of engineers and marketing people, and cut the time spent in politicking.

Even small changes in scale, up or down, can create a significant competitive advantage. The business magazine the *Economist* is a great example. The *Economist* patches its editorial staff into larger chunks of scope than its rival *Business Week*. This means that the *Economist* publishes a similar magazine, but with a smaller number of departments and fewer writers. Having fewer writers lets the *Economist* pay higher salaries to attract the most talented ones. This creates a virtuous cycle in which writers cover lots of different issues and industries and so are able to write the more insightful, varied, and creative stories that characterize the magazine. These engaging and sophisticated stories have attracted an increasing number of readers, and the *Economist* is gaining market share. And, since these readers tend to be wealthy businesspeople, advertising revenues and profits have grown even faster.

The uncertainty of a market also affects optimal patch size. As a rule of thumb, more turbulent markets favor focus and agility—and hence small size—whereas more static markets favor economies of scale—and hence large size. For example, the Danish bank Lan & Spar set up a new business unit to enter the emergent at-home banking market. Because the business was free-standing, bank employees could more easily think beyond the constraints of traditional banking. But in about two years—when the at-home service was established as a separate business with a clear value proposition—it was recombined with the traditional business to gain scale economies and offer an integrated service.[3]

Because the edge between agility and efficiency in business unit size shifts as markets evolve, patching managers must track the subtle shifts along that edge closely. Consider Dell again. The Internet and multimedia technologies have created extreme turbulence in computing and altered the balance from efficiency toward agility. In response, Dell's managers have shifted their patch size. They have not only created more patches in recent years, but they have also cut their average patch size (as measured by revenues) despite the company's overall growth. As a result, Dell has been able to finely tune product offerings, sales approaches, and profit levers in customer service, and by doing so has achieved extraordinary financial performance. (For information on repatching, see "Is It Time to Repatch?" at the end of this article.)

Laying the Groundwork

Patching won't work unless the company's infrastructure supports the process. That requires modularity, detailed and complete business-level metrics, and consistent companywide compensation.

Modularity is the most important of these elements. A patching company's business units need to be focused and discrete so that they can be combined seamlessly. A complicated organizational structure—in particular, one with lots of shared services or cross-business committees—will slow patching down. Often the modular structure is replicated within the business units of patching companies in the form of focused, semiautonomous teams. For example, managers at Sun Microsystems organize their company into discrete business units that they call planets and then into focused product teams within them.

Complete and detailed business-level metrics that are comparable across businesses—on revenue, gross margin, customer preferences, product development time, and costs—are also essential for effective patching. Such metrics and their trends give corporate managers in-depth knowledge of their businesses and can help them predict how and when to repatch. A good example is Honda. By carefully monitoring consumer preferences, Honda's managers patched their recreational vehicle offerings in Japan into product lines that crossed traditional categories but that were closer to consumer preferences. The Odyssey, for instance, is part station wagon and part minivan. That patching move allowed Honda to take major market share away from Toyota.

Fine-grained metrics are particularly useful for helping managers pull apart misleading, aggregate numbers. A European hospitality company, for example, was organized into one large, vertically integrated business that included brewing, pub, and hotel operations. Managers had no way to consider the very different operations as separate businesses. Only when new metrics allowed managers to understand the different business models of each operation were they able to repatch effectively. They ended up splitting the hotel and pub operations into separate business units and selling off the less profitable brewery business.

Incomplete or inaccurate metrics make patching impossible to do well. For example, managers at a steel minimill lacked basic measures such as regional sales growth rates, how plant efficiency changed with volume, costs associated with different kinds of customers, and product profitability. With considerable effort, the managers gathered these numbers for a major restructuring. But because such metrics were not routinely accessible, these managers couldn't conceive of patching on an ongoing basis.

Companywide compensation parity is the final infrastructure component of patching companies. After all, patching requires the movement of people, and inconsistent compensation can erect barriers to that movement. Managers at a major U.S. bank learned that lesson the hard way. They created a subsidiary to tackle nontraditional branch-banking in grocery stores, pharmacies, and so forth. They planned to revitalize the old branch banking business with lessons from the nontraditional branches. But the new business paid much better than the older one, which created a serious (albeit predictable) problem: no one wanted to leave the new business.

Principles for Patching Well

If senior executives adopt the patching mind-set—in other words, if they assume that organizational change is frequent, routine, and mostly small in scale—and also develop an infrastructure that supports a fluid organization, then they can start to patch as market opportunities arise. (See "New Executive Role Creates Corporate Value" at the end of this article.) The companies we studied patched in remarkably similar ways. In fact, we detected some patterns so common that we call them principles.

DO IT FAST

Patching decisions are best made quickly—in two or three months at most. Fast choices reduce anxiety and politicking. Drawn-out restructuring decisions are lightning rods for negative emotions. In fact, one reason reorganizations in traditional companies are politically charged is that managers take so long to decide things because they know that restructuring is rare. In companies that patch, however, politicking is mitigated since no one expects any particular patch to last forever. Minimization of politics further contributes to the speed and efficiency of the patching process.

DEVELOP MULTIPLE OPTIONS, THEN MAKE A ROUGHLY RIGHT CHOICE

When a patching occasion arises, managers instinctively focus on one response and analyze it thoroughly—but that process is too slow. Effective patchers develop three or four alternatives. This is surprisingly easy to do. In fact, patchers can often generate several options in a few hours. Managers can then analyze these options quickly for two reasons: it is cognitively easier to compare several alternatives than to analyze a single alternative in depth, and the crucial factors like business model similarity and P&L viability are usually clear.

An example from a major printing company, which we'll call PrintCo, illustrates this process. PrintCo faced a typical patching situation: both the book division and the catalog division had begun exploring a new market opportunity—digital print technology—at about the same time. Eventually, PrintCo's managers recognized the overlap and the need to patch. They developed several possible options in less than a week. Option 1 was to create a stand-alone digital printing division. Option 2 was to anchor digital printing in the book division. Option 3 was to put it in the catalog division. Option 4 was to maintain the status quo.

PrintCo's executives quickly rejected the first option because there was insufficient revenue to make it a financially viable stand-alone business unit. Business unit size was the deciding factor here. They also rejected option 4 because it spread resources too thinly across the two divisions.

The choice between options 2 and 3 was less straight-forward. On the one hand, the book division was further along in developing a business case for digital printing. It was also larger, better established, and more able to fund a new venture. On the other hand, its plate was very full, so digital technology wouldn't be the first priority. In addition, digital printing didn't offer book customers immediate benefits. Books have very long, standardized press runs, but digital technology is most promising for short, customized runs.

The catalog division would have more trouble build-ing a new business since it had fewer resources, but it also had more to gain from the opportunity. Digital tech-nology presented a chance to develop employees' techni-cal skills in a potentially valuable emerging technology.

Creating "shadow organizations" lets managers test how well various aspects of a patch will work.

In addition, PrintCo's man-agers believed that a combina-tion of traditional and digital print technologies could create exceptional value for catalog customers, who could order customized versions if digital printing was available. Therefore, PrintCo might gain market share in a business that it had entered late. The clincher was that adding digital printing to the catalog business would build employment in a geographic region where it was needed. PrintCo's managers went with option 3.

TAKE AN ORGANIZATIONAL TEST-DRIVE

Rather than painstakingly plan out the details in
advance, savvy patchers prototype new patches before
they make a final decision. This test-drive speeds up
analysis and lowers the chances of major errors, just as it
would in new product development.

One common tactic is to create temporary "shadow
organizations" within the existing business infrastructure. This approach lets managers test how well various
aspects of a patch will work. An enterprise software company we'll call SavvySystems is a good illustration. The
electronics business unit served telecommunications,
semiconductor, and computer customers. SavvySystems
was growing rapidly, and management was preoccupied
dealing with high growth and with several demanding
computer customers. As a result, it was shortchanging
opportunities in the telecommunications and semiconductor markets. Management tentatively decided to split
the electronics division into three distinct business units
corresponding to the company's three customer groups.
But before finalizing their choice, managers created a
shadow organization to test-drive the proposed patching
solution.

First, they checked financial viability by installing
P&L metrics for each proposed new business and letting the units run against the new metrics. Each turned
out to be financially sound. Next, managers tested the
proposed patches from a product-development point of
view. They split product developers into three groups
that mirrored the proposed new patches, but they kept
those discrete groups within the electronics business
unit. This shadow organization revealed that, from a
product development perspective, it made sense to

combine its telecommunications and computing hardware customers, which had similar enterprise software
requirements, but to split computing software and
semiconductors into separate businesses. So SavvySystems realigned the product development staff and the
P&Ls, but the changes still had not been made formally.
In a third test, managers divided customer support into
three groups that mirrored the latest patching option.
Several client companies were then shuffled between
business buckets because of unexpected customer support demands that the shadow organization revealed.
SavvySystems' managers then formally repatched the
electronics business—with few post-split headaches.
They ended up with three new business units: telecommunications and computing hardware, computing software, and semiconductors.

GET THE GENERAL MANAGER RIGHT

Selecting the appropriate general manager for the business unit is also essential for effective patching. Choosing the wrong manager—or having no appropriate manager available—can instantly stall patching. Executives
from Hewlett-Packard's printers business were particularly skilled at making unusual yet effective selections
and keeping the pipeline of good managers filled. Here's
an example.

In the mid-1990s, HP's managers planned to transfer a
large-format printer business from a San Diego business
unit to one in Barcelona. The large-format business was
maturing and needed greater manufacturing efficiency.
The unit in Barcelona was better suited to improving efficiency. The one in San Diego was regarded as being strong
in innovation, and so it would start a new business. The

transfer created emotional upheaval, especially in San Diego. The choice of general manager was crucial to making the patch succeed. In an unexpected switch, the general manager in Barcelona was moved to San Diego. He had the ideal perspective because he was in a unique position to understand all of the players. Because he knew how anxious the Spaniards were to begin running the business, he accelerated some aspects of the transfer. But because he now had to manage a start-up in San Diego and knew that it would take time to launch a new business, he slowed down other aspects of the transfer. Simultaneously, an American with high general-management potential was moved to the smaller Barcelona operation. This placement helped bridge the cultural gap between the two divisions and gave the new general manager valuable experience.

SCRIPT THE DETAILS

After the decision has been made on the new patch, the main concern is ensuring that the work itself doesn't get neglected in the confusion of complicated organizational change. That may involve keeping a development project moving, say, or making sure customers don't fall through the cracks. Successful patchers follow a script after the patching is announced. Laying out a detailed plan— sometimes even specifying day-by-day activities for the first 30 to 60 days—helps to coordinate the many tasks and people involved in the patch. The specifics of the plan are actually somewhat arbitrary. Some patching companies have SWAT teams that swing into action to provide extra support; others use checklists of major activities. The key is to have the template ready.

An essential part of the script is to push managers to reach financial and other goals (for example, customer acquisition targets and project deadlines) quickly. The reasons for this are mostly emotional. Patching creates anxiety and even hard feelings, especially in difficult situations such as combining previously distinct businesses, transferring from one business unit to another, or adding businesses through acquisitions. If people focus quickly on clear goals, then they spend more time looking toward the future and less time stewing about the past. GE Capital's managers choreograph acquisitions very tightly for that reason. They have found that the sooner their acquired groups focus on delivering the numbers, the sooner they get integrated into the new organization.

Another component of the template is recognizing and rewarding managers whose businesses are split, exited, or combined. Such moves usually cause emotional upheaval, and so explicitly recognizing the managers' contribution to the company is an important part of effective patching.

Common Stumbling Blocks

Even the best managers make patching mistakes now and then. A common one is to violate the modularity of the businesses. We call this "missing the hill," and it happens when responsibility for tackling a particular product or market area is not given to one unit. Consider the case of a computer company we studied. The general managers of two businesses independently spotted the same opportunity to create software that measured the performance of computer systems. This was simply a collision of two businesses into the same market space. Both general managers made a compelling case for keeping the business within their own domain. With the agreement of the two division heads, the patching executive decided to split the option across the two units. He gave the product development lead to one business unit and the marketing and profit responsibility to the other. He reasoned that the first business unit would benefit from developing the technical skill set, but that the business opportunity was a better fit with the second. With all managers in agreement, success seemed like a sure thing. A couple of months later, however, it became clear that no one felt responsible for the new product line. Formal responsibility had been given to an overworked lower-level manager who lacked the time and the status to make things happen. The new venture fell through the crack between two very big businesses.

Allowing one business unit to become much larger than the related businesses is another common stumbling block. We call it "Snow White and the Seven Dwarfs." Typically, the general manager of the large business becomes too powerful. That creates awkward and often dysfunctional decision-making dynamics and sometimes even undercuts the power of the patching executive. Business decisions tend to favor Snow White, even though that may not represent the best future opportunities of the collective businesses.

Those mistakes and others do occur, even in the most sophisticated patching companies. In fact, mistakes are to be expected when managers balance on the edge between agility and efficiency. The key is quick correction. For example, the patching executive in the computer company described earlier recognized the mistake and, within several months, repatched the new software business into a focused division.

The clear-cut partitioning of businesses into neat, equidistant rectangles on an organizational chart becomes out of date.

Is Patching in Your Future?

In turbulent markets, businesses and opportunities are constantly falling out of alignment. New technologies, novel products and services, and emerging markets create fresh opportunities. Converging markets produce more. And of course, some markets fade. As a result, the clear-cut partitioning of businesses into neat, equidistant rectangles on an organizational chart becomes out of date as opportunities come and go, collide and separate, grow and shrink.

In this landscape of continuous flux, corporate-level strategists must continually remap their businesses to market opportunities. Patching is the best way we know to tackle this crucial task. For managers in dynamic markets, then, patching becomes an enormously important skill to add to the corporate repertoire. Corporations that don't learn to patch are asking their employees to compete with the handicap of a misaligned organization.

The New Corporate Strategy

TRADITIONAL CORPORATE STRATEGY emphasizes strategic positioning. That is, senior executives create a defensible strategic position by acquiring or building valuable assets, wisely allocating resources to them, and weaving synergies among them. As part of creating that positioning, these executives set the size, boundaries, and scope of the company. And they ensure that business units have winning strategies. The result is supposed to be sustained competitive advantage and superior, long-term performance.

In reality, traditional corporate strategy often fails. Managers frequently pay too much for acquisitions. Synergies don't happen very often. Diversification beyond one or two SIC codes stalls. Business unit strategies are quickly outdated. Competitive advantage is rarely sustained for more than a few years. But this dismal record does not suggest that the corporation adds no value beyond the sum of its businesses. Rather, it demonstrates that the traditional concept of corporate strategy is leading many managers astray.

Especially in volatile markets, corporate strategy should center on *strategic processes* more than on *strategic positioning*. In these markets, it is impossible to predict which competencies or strategies will be successful and for how long. The implication is that it's more important to build corporate-level strategic processes that enable dynamic strategic repositioning than it is to build any particular defensible position.

But these strategic processes are not just accelerated versions of traditional corporate processes. It's not strategic planning on steroids. Traditional planning and resource allocation are too top-down and are focused on control. In contrast, the new corporate-level strategic processes center on change. They add economic value by enabling managers to mobilize and reconfigure corporate resources to capture market opportunities faster than the competition. One of these newly defined processes is patching.

The payoff from the new corporate strategy is significant, especially in dynamic markets. Why? Business units in those markets are configured in small chunks to give them agility. The more uncertain the market, the smaller the chunks. In fact, even entrepreneurial ventures are often structured into multiple businesses in this kind of market. As a result, there are more business units in the corporation to coordinate, more need to offset scale disadvantages by capturing synergies, and more volatility around scope and boundary decisions. In other words, corporate strategy—reinvented to focus more on processes than on positioning—is even more essential in dynamic markets than it is in static ones.

Is It Time to Repatch?

1. Are your businesses ignoring significant opportunities? Conversely, are they converging onto the same new market opportunities?

2. Has growth stalled in your current patching arrangement? That is, is your average selling price, market share, gross margin, or rate of new customer acquisition stagnant or falling? Or is your cost structure higher than your competition's?

3. Are you imposing one management structure on your businesses that evolve at different rates (that is, some are operating on Internet time and others are more stable)?

4. Are your customers segmenting your products or services by, for example, product features, distribution channel, level of support, or type of technology, but you aren't?

5. Are better performing competitors patched differently than you are? Is it an advantage for them?

New Executive Role Creates Corporate Value

PATCHING EXECUTIVES—the multibusiness managers who match their businesses with shifting markets on an ongoing basis—make a unique contribution to the value of the corporation. They accomplish what cannot be readily done at the business-unit level. Because they fly at a higher altitude than business-level managers, they are better able to see patching moves since they're more attuned to broad market trends. Patching executives can also orchestrate moves that would be painful for business-level managers to make because they involve exits from current businesses, transfers, and combinations of existing businesses.

Patching executives also accomplish things that investors in the financial markets could not. The markets permit investors to make simple moves like adding and removing businesses from a portfolio. But markets do not allow investors the full repertoire of moves—such as combining businesses, splitting them apart, transferring pieces from one business to another, and raising the orbit of multiple pieces into one business. Also, markets provide neither the fine-grained, organizational metrics to spot patching opportunities nor the routines to execute patches quickly.

Great patching executives all possess one critical skill: pattern recognition. Simply put, they can see trends developing in the marketplace before most other people can. In part, they rely on high-quality metrics to aid their foresight and reinforce their intuition. More significant, they have a deep understanding of two concrete aspects of managing: *market segmentation*, which reveals how to optimally configure patches to exploit market opportunities, and *road maps* for new products, services, or technologies, which suggest how future patches are likely to evolve. Thus, patching executives "define the firm" not only in the traditional, external terms of boundaries, scope, and scale but also in the new, internal terms of dynamic business patching.

Chaos, Complexity Theory, and Patching

CHAOS THEORY DESCRIBES HOW seemingly small changes in one place can create large and often unpredictable changes in distant places. But although chaos theory reveals why markets with frequent change are so challenging to manage, it doesn't give executives much practical insight about what to do. That's where complexity theory comes into the picture. Complexity theory focuses on the capacity of a system (organizations, countries, or even beehives) to adapt to chaotic turbulence—in the context of this article, a multibusiness company's capacity to adapt to fast-changing markets.

There's now considerable evidence from complexity theory to suggest that adaptation is most effective in systems whose pieces are connected, but only *partially* connected. The argument is that too rigid an organizational structure will create obstructions, whereas too loose a structure will create chaos. Consider, for example, the use of traffic lights in a town. Without any lights, traffic would be chaotic, but too many lights would cause gridlock. A moderate number of lights creates some structure but allows drivers to adapt their routes in surprising ways to changing traffic conditions. Thus the key to effective adaptation is to stay poised on the edge of chaos.

Patching managers are poised on that edge in two ways. First, they pay a great deal of attention to the size of their business units, trading the adaptability and focus of small size against the efficiencies of large size. Second, they make individual businesses modular, but not completely autonomous. They centrally control the unit's size, content and proximity to other units, but they simultaneously permit specific strategies to emerge from the individual businesses.

Notes

1. Research by INSEAD professor Charles Galunic and by Stuart Kauffman of the Bios Group was important to our recognition of patching.

2. This example is drawn from Mehrdad Berghai, Stephen Coley, and David White's *The Alchemy of Growth* (Perseus Books, 1999).

3. Costas Markides of the London Business School provided this example.

Originally published in May–June 1999
Reprint 99303

About the Contributors

JOSEPH L. BADARACCO, JR., is the John Shad Professor of
Business Ethics at Harvard Business School. He teaches
courses on strategy, general management, and business ethics
in the School's M.B.A. and executive programs. Badaracco is a
graduate of St. Louis University, Oxford University, where he
was a Rhodes Scholar, and Harvard Business School, where he
earned an M.B.A. and a D.B.A. Badaracco is also Faculty Chair
for the M.B.A. Elective Curriculum and the past chairman of
the Harvard University Advisory Committee on Shareholder
Responsibility. Professor Badaracco has taught in executive
programs in the United States, Japan, and several other countries. He is a director of Excelon Corporation and faculty chair
of the Nomura School of Advanced Management in Tokyo. He
is the author of *Loading the Dice, Leadership and the Quest for
Integrity, The Knowledge Link, Business Ethics: Roles and
Responsibilities*, and *Defining Moments: When Managers Must
Choose between Right and Right*. These books have been trans-
lated into nine languages. His latest book, published in Febru-
ary 2002, is *Leading Quietly: An Unorthodox Guide to Doing
the Right Thing*.

SHONA L. BROWN is a partner in the Los Angeles office of
McKinsey and Company, where she has served technology
and media clients extensively on strategy development, business model transformation, go-to-market strategy, and a full

range of business building and change management issues. She is a leader of McKinsey's Strategy Practice and has written extensively on strategy issues, including the Harvard Business School Press book *Competing on the Edge: Strategy as Structured Chaos*. Before joining McKinsey, Brown completed a Ph.D. and post-doctorate at Stanford University in strategy and technology management. She also holds an M.A. in Economics and Philosophy from Oxford University, which she earned while studying as a Rhodes Scholar, and a B.Eng. in Systems and Computer engineering from Carleton University in Canada.

TOM COPELAND is Managing Director of Corporate Finance at the Monitor Group in Cambridge, Massachusetts. As a consultant, he has served over 200 companies in thirty-four countries over a fifteen-year career, starting in 1987 as partner and co-leader of McKinsey's global corporate finance practice for eleven years. He is experienced in mergers and acquisitions, real options, risk management, performance measurement systems, and corporate restructuring and financing. As an academic, Tom earned his Ph.D. and M.B.A. from the Wharton School, was a full tenured professor of finance at UCLA, and an adjunct professor of finance at New York University, Massachusetts Institute of Technology, and Harvard Business School. He is coauthor of *Valuation: Measuring and Managing the Value of Companies*, *Financial Theory and Corporate Policy*, *Real Options: A Practitioner's Guide*, and *Managerial Finance*.

DIANE L. COUTU is a senior editor at *Harvard Business Review* who specializes in articles on psychology and business. Before coming to HBR, she worked as a communications specialist for McKinsey and Company, the global management consultancy, and as a foreign correspondent for *Time Maga-*

zine and *The Wall Street Journal Europe.* She studied literature at Yale and economics at Oxford University, where she was a Rhodes Scholar. Most recently, she was an Affiliate Scholar and a Silberger Fellow at The Boston Psychoanalytic Society and Institute, Inc.

At the time this article was originally published, KATHLEEN M. EISENHARDT was a professor of strategy and organization at Stanford University in Stanford, California.

DAVID N. JAMES began his career with Lloyds Bank before moving at age twenty-six to Ford Motor Credit, where he spent ten progressive years in European operations. Following Ford, James moved to the Rank Organization, where he was successive CEO of three of their trouble-hit subsidiaries. Having developed a taste for rescue work, he then set up his own operations in 1982. Since then he has handled a series of high profile corporate crisis, usually acting as Executive Chairman and CEO. These have included the conglomerates Central and Sherwood plc, Eagle Trust plc, and North Sea Assets plc as well as Davies and Newman plc (Dan-Air), British Shoe Corporation, and The Robinson Group. More recently, he was drafted in as Chairman to resolve the problems afflicting New Millennium Experience Company, the government-backed company responsible for the Greenwich Millennium Dome.

DARRELL RIGBY is a director in the Boston office of Bain & Company, a global management consulting firm. He is the head of Bain's worldwide retail practice, and leads the firm's research on "Winning in Turbulence"—examining the long-term results of management actions taken during economic downturns. In 1993, Mr. Rigby founded Bain's global survey on "Management Tools and Trends," which is widely cited in the business pages of U.S. and international publications.

"Moving Upward in a Downturn" is the first of four articles on vanguard corporate strategies that Mr. Rigby published in *Harvard Business Review* in 2001–02.

ADRIAN J. SLYWOTZKY is a Vice President and member of the Board of Directors of Mercer Management Consulting, Inc., a global strategy consulting firm. Mr. Slywotzky directs Mercer's intellectual capital development and consults extensively at the CEO level on issues relating to new business development and creating new areas of value growth. He is the author of *The Art of Profitability* and *Value Migration*, and is the coauthor of *The Profit Zone*, *Profit Patterns*, and *How Digital Is Your Business?* A frequent speaker on business strategy and business design, Mr. Slywotzky has been featured at the World Economic Forum in Davos, Switzerland, and has been a keynote speaker at the Microsoft CEO Summit and the *Forbes*, *Fortune*, and *Business Week* CEO Conferences. He holds degrees from Harvard College, Harvard Law School, and Harvard Business School.

At the time this article was originally published, SUZY WETLAUFER was a senior editor at *Harvard Business Review*.

RICHARD WISE leads Mercer Management Consulting's North American strategy practice. He has particular expertise in helping large companies identify, prioritize, and exploit new growth opportunities through innovative business designs. Mr. Wise has worked with leading companies in the automotive, manufacturing, financial services, retail, software, and materials industries, among others. Mr. Wise played a key role in developing Mercer's Value-Driven Business Design process for systematically identifying and exploiting opportunities for companies to create shareholder value growth. He was a significant contributor to Mercer's recent books on growth strategy, *Value Migration*, *The Profit Zone*, and *Profit*

Patterns. Mr. Wise speaks frequently on winning growth strategies and value migration. His most recent articles include "Secret to a Long Life in Tech? Understanding Customer Needs" in *Investor's Business Daily* and "Go Downstream: The New Profit Imperative in Manufacturing," which appeared in *Harvard Business Review.* Mr. Wise holds a B.A. from the University of Pennsylvania and an M.B.A. from the Wharton School.

Index